THI
INFLUENCE OF BUDDHISM
ON
PRIMITIVE CHRISTIANITY

THE INFLUENCE OF BUDDHISM ON PRIMITIVE CHRISTIANITY

ARTHUR LILLIE

GYAN

Published by

Gyan Publishing House
5, Ansari Road
Daryaganj, New Delhi-110002
Phone: 011-47034999, 9811692060
E-mail: books@gyanbooks.com

Distribution Network
gyanbooks.com
India, USA, Canada, UK, Australia

ISBN: 978-93-6920-149-5 (PB)

First Published, 1893

2nd Impression 2025

Printed at: Gyan Press, Delhi.

THE INFLUENCE OF BUDDHISM ON PRIMITIVE CHRISTIANITY
Author: ARTHUR LILLIE

THE INFLUENCE OF BUDDHISM

ON

PRIMITIVE CHRISTIANITY

By the same Author,

BUDDHISM IN CHRISTENDOM.

"The most learned, thoughtful, and thought-provoking work which has yet appeared on this momentous question. . . . I read the book from cover to cover with much interest."—*Truth.*

"The present work is of the profoundest interest, and is certain to command attention in all future discussions of the subject with which it deals. . . . It is exceedingly ably written."—*Scotsman.*

"The relation of Essenism to Buddhism is here dwelt upon with some fresh illustration of the probably Indian origin of the Therapeuts of Alexandria. Mr. Lillie's chapters on ritual and observances are rendered attractive by a number of interesting illustrations."—*Athenæum.*

"Discusses the influence which Buddhism has had on Christianity. The admission that there is any relationship at all between the two will be vehemently denied by many good people, but no one can impartially and fairly study Mr. Lillie's book, examine his evidence, and give due weight to his arguments, without admitting that the connection not only exists but is an intimate one."—*Evening Standard.*

Also,

THE POPULAR LIFE OF BUDDHA.

"Contends that the atheistic and soulless Buddhism was drawn from the 'Great Vehicle,' which was a spurious system introduced about the time of the Christian era, whereas the 'Little Vehicle,' compiled by Asoka, contained the motto, 'Confess and believe in God.' There are a large number of passages drawn from the sacred books, which tend to prove that Mr. Lillie is right in his theory of Buddhist theology. Even Dr. Rhys Davids admits that the Cakkavati Buddha was to early Buddhists what the Messiah Logos was to early Christians. 'If this be so,' as Mr. Lillie is justified in asking, how can an atheist believe in a 'Word of God made flesh?'

"Mr. Lillie thus sums up the originalities of the Buddhist movement:—Enforced vegetarianism for the whole nation; enforced abstinence from wine; abolition of slavery: the introduction of the principle of forgiveness of injuries in opposition to the *lex talionis;* uncompromising antagonism to all national religious rites that were opposed to the *gnosis* or spiritual development of the individual; beggary, continence, and asceticism for religious teachers."—*Spectator.*

"Contains many quotations from the Buddhist religious writings, which are beautiful and profound—a most readable book."—*Saturday Review.*

"Our author has unquestionably the story-teller's gift."—*St. James Gazette.*

THE INFLUENCE OF BUDDHISM ON PRIMITIVE CHRISTIANITY

BY

ARTHUR LILLIE

AUTHOR OF "BUDDHISM IN CHRISTENDOM," ETC.

LONDON

SWAN SONNENSCHEIN & CO.

NEW YORK: CHARLES SCRIBNER'S SONS

1893

PREFACE.

A VOLUME that proves that much of the New Testament is parable rather than history will shock many readers, but from the days of Origen and Clement of Alexandria to the days of Swedenborg the same thing has been affirmed. The proof that this parabolic writing has been derived from a previous religion will shock many more. The biographer of Christ has one sole duty, namely, to produce the actual historical Jesus. In the New Testament there are two Christs, an Essene and an anti-Essene Christ, and all modern biographers who have sought to combine the two have failed necessarily. It is the contention of this work that Christ was an Essene monk; that Christianity was Essenism; and that Essenism was due, as Dean Mansel contended, to the Buddhist missionaries "who visited Egypt within two generations of the time of Alexander the Great." ("Gnostic Heresies," p. 31.)

The Reformation, in the view of Macaulay, was the struggle of layman *versus* monk. In consequence, many good Protestants are shocked to hear such a term applied to the founder of their creed. But here I must point out one fact. In the Essene monasteries, as in the Buddhist, there was no life vow. This made the monastery less a career than a school for spiritual initiation. In modern monasteries St. John of the Cross can dream sweet dreams of God in one cell, and his neighbour may be Friar Tuck, but to both the monastery is a prison. This alters the complexion of the celibacy question, and so does the fact that the Christians were fighting a mighty battle with the priesthoods.

The Son of Man envied the security of the crannies of the "fox." He called his opponents "wolves." His flock after his death met with closed doors for fear of the Jews. The "pure gospel," says the Clementine Homilies (ch. ii. 17), was "sent abroad secretly" after the removal to Pella. The new sect, not as Christians but as Essenes, were tortured, killed, hunted down. To such, "two coats," "wives," daily wine celebrations were scarcely fitted.

Twice has Buddhism invaded the West, once at

the birth of Christianity, and once when the Templars brought home from Palestine Cabbalism, Sufism, Freemasonry. And our zealous missionaries in Ceylon and elsewhere, by actively translating Buddhist books to refute them, have produced a result which is a little startling. Once more Buddhism is advancing with giant strides. Germany, America, England are overrun with it. M. Léon de Rosny, a professor of the Sorbonne, announces that in Paris there are 30,000 Buddhists at least. A French frigate came back from China the other day with one-third of the crew converted Buddhists. Schopenhauer admits that he got the philosophy which now floods Germany from a perusal of English translations of Buddhist books. Even the nonsense of Madame Blavatsky has a little genuine Buddhism at the bottom, which gives it a brief life.

The religions of earth mean strife and partisan watch-cries, partisan symbols, partisan gestures, partisan clothes. But as the daring climber mounts the cool steep, the anathemas of priests fall faintly on the ear, and the largest cathedrals grow dim, in a pure region where Wesley and Fenelon, Mirza the Sufi and Swedenborg, Spinoza and Amiel, can shake hands. If this new study of Buddhism has shown that the two great Teachers of the world taught much the same doctrine, we have distinctly a gain and not a loss. That religion was the religion of the individual, as discriminated from religion by body corporate.

CONTENTS.

INFLUENCE OF BUDDHISM ON CHRISTIANITY

INTRODUCTORY.

In the *Revue des Deus Mondes*, July 15th, 1888, M. Emile Burnouf has an article entitled "Le Bouddhisme en Occident."

M. Burnouf holds that the Christianity of the Council of Nice was due to a conflict between the Aryan and the Semite, between Buddhism and Mosaism :—

"History and comparative mythology are teaching every day more plainly that creeds grow slowly up. None come into the world ready-made, and as if by magic. The origin of events is lost in the infinite. A great Indian poet has said, 'The beginning of things evades us; their end evades us also. We see only the middle.'"

M. Burnouf asserts that the Indian origin of Christianity is no longer contested : "It has been placed in full light by the researches of scholars, and notably English scholars, and by the publication of the original texts. . . . In point of fact, for a long time, folks had been struck with the resemblances, or rather the identical elements contained in Christianity, and Buddhism. Writers of the firmest faith and most sincere piety have admitted them. In the last century these analogies were set down to the Nestorians, but since then the science of Oriental chronology has come into being, and proved that Buddha is many years anterior to Nestorius and Jesus. Thus the Nestorian theory had to be given up. But a thing may be posterior to another without proving derivation. So the problem remained unsolved until recently, when the pathway that Buddhism followed was traced, step by step, from India to Jerusalem."

What are the facts upon which scholars abroad are basing the conclusions here announced? I have been asked by the present publishers to give a short and popular answer to this question. The theory of this book, stated in a few words, is that at the date of King Asoka (B.C. 260), Persia, Greece, Egypt, Palestine had been powerfully influenced by Buddhist propagandism.

Buddha, as we know from the Rupnath Rock inscription, died 470 years before Christ. He announced before he died that his Dharma would endure five hundred years. (Oldenburg, "Buddhism," p. 327.) He announced also that his successor would be Maitreya, the Buddha of "Brotherly Love." In consequence, at the date of the Christian era, many lands were on the tip-toe of expectation. "According to the prophecy of Zoradascht," says the First Gospel of the Infancy, "the wise men came to Palestine, expecting, probably, Craosha, as the Jews expected Messiah. The time passed. Jesus was executed.

His followers dispersed in consternation. The conception that he was the real Messiah was apparently long in taking definite form.

First came a book of "sayings" only. Then a gospel was constructed—the Gospel of the Hebrews—of which only a small fragment can be restored. This was the basis of many other gospels. At the date of Irenæus (180 A.D.) they were very numerous. (Hœr i. 19.) As only the Old Testament, at that time, was considered the Bible, the composers of these gospels apparently thought it no great sin to draw on the Alexandrine library of Buddhist books for much of their matter, it being a maxim of both the Essenes and the early Christians that a holy book was more allegory than history.

But before I compare the Buddhist and Christian narratives, I must say a word about the early religion of the Jews.

CHAPTER I.

Moses.

UNTIL within the last forty years the Old Testament has been practically a sealed book.

It found interpreters, no doubt—two great groups.

The first group pointed to its useless and arbitrary edicts, and pronounced them the inventions of priests inspired by fraud and greed.

The second group practically admitted the arbitrary and useless nature of most of the edicts, but maintained that they were given by the All-wise, in a book penned by His finger, to miraculously prepare a nation distinct from the other nations of the earth, for a special purpose. They were "types" of a higher revelation, a "better covenant."

Practically, with both of these interpreters Mosaism was a pure comedy.

But comparative mythology, unborn yesterday, is telling a different story. It shows that the religion of the Jews, far from having been a distinct religion miraculously given to a peculiar people, had the same rites and gods as the creeds of its Semitic neighbours. It shows us these Semites, or descendants of Shem, in two great groups, differing much in language and religion. It shows us the southern Semites, the Arabs, the Himyarites, the Ethiopians. It shows us the northern group, the Babylonians or Chaldeans, the Assyrians, the Arameans, the Canaanites, the Hebrews. It shows us their gods, El and Yahve, and Astarte of Sidon; and going a step back shows how the Semites borrowed from an earlier civilisation, that of the Acadians, the yellow-faced Mongols who seem to have preceded the white races everywhere. "The Semite borrowed the old Acadian pantheon *en bloc*," says Professor Sayce ("Ancient Empires," p. 151).

But the work of the archæologist and the anthropologist has been still more important.

The former has suddenly revealed to us chapters in the history of human experience hitherto undreamt of. He has allowed us to peer far, far into the past, to see man at an incalculable distance.

Thousands and thousands of years before Cain and Abel we see the palæolithic man, "dolichocephalic and with prominent jaws," pursue the great migrations of urus, reindeer, mammoth, and the thick-nose rhinoceros from Cumberland to Algeria, and Algeria to Cumberland, passing dry-shod to France, and from Sicily to Africa. He is naked. He is armed with a javelin with a flint head. He is an animal, struggling for survival with other animals. He eats his foes as wolves eat vanquished wolves. To extract the marrow from their bones he cracks them with his poor flint "celt" or "*langue du chat;*" and these cracked human bones 240,000 years afterwards are found in caves and in beds of gravel and sand, and brick earth, and tell their story. Some are charred, which proves that the notion of sacrifice to an unseen being was due to him.

To this poor savage our debt is quite incalculable.

1. He invented the missile. This made the monkey dominant in the animal world. He became a man.

2. He invented religion.

Here the valuable work of the anthropologist chimes in. He has collected the records of ancient and modern savages, and compared them with the records of caves and beds of gravel. In this way he has allowed us to peer into the mind of the stone-using savage, who lived at least 240,000 years ago. And the Bible of the Jews, from being a text-book for sermons which bewildered the moral sense even of children, has become, for the study of the great evolution of religion, one of the most valuable books in the world. It bridges the gap between the neolithic or polished-stone-using man and Christ and Mahomet.

Before we go further, let us say a word about the authorship of the Old Testament.

The Books of Moses were compiled by Ezra, at the date of Artaxerxes, the King of the Persians.

It is to be observed that this is not an extravagant guess of German theorists. It is stated authoritatively by Clement of Alexandria. (Strom. i. 22.) Irenæus, Tertullian, Eusebius, Jerome, and Basil give the same testimony. But a greater authority is behind. It is known that Christ and His disciples, and the early fathers, used the Septuagint or Greek version of the Bible, and Dr. Giles goes so far as to say that there is no hint amongst the latter of the knowledge of even the existence of the Hebrew version. In this Bible (2 Esdras xiv.), it is announced distinctly that the "law was burnt;" and that Ezra, aided by the Holy Ghost and "wonderful visions of the night," wrote down "all that hath been done in the world from the beginning which was written in thy law."

Let us write down a few dates from the accepted chronology.

	B.C.
Adam	**4004**
Abraham	**1996**
Moses	**1571**
Nebuchadnezzar leads Jews in captivity to Babylon	**587**
Jews restored	**517**
Ezra	**457**

Thus the story of Adam in its present form was written down 3547 years after it had occurred. The story of Abraham was written down 1539 years after it occurred. The transactions between Yahve and Moses were written down 1114 years after they occurred.

To gauge the full significance of this, let us call to mind that the poet Tennyson a few years back compiled from old ballads and chronicles the story of Arthur, a king separated from him by about the same gap of time that parted Ezra and Moses. The poet was honest, according to our ideas of honesty, and sought to give a faithful picture of Arthur's court—with a success that is only moderate. But Ezra was not honest, that is, in our sense of the word. His nation had been a captive of the Babylonians, and had been released from slavery and the lash by Cyrus. In consequence, the molten bulls of the temples of the Jewish taskmasters stank in his nostrils, and led him to advocate the severe nakedness of the Persian fire-altar. And he proposed to do this, not so much by writing new books as by altering the old records and legends, and proclaiming his views through the mouths of the time-honoured patriarchs.

But all this involved a grotesque inference that he seems not to have anticipated. If Abraham, Jacob, Moses, Solomon, knew in their secret hearts that the one fierce hatred of Yahve was the graven image, their assiduous idolatry spread over 1500 years must have been a pure comedy, intended to insult Yahve, not to conciliate him.

What is the object of the religion of the savage? Anthropology has recently answered this question.

The religion of the savage is a slavish reign of terror. His rites and prohibitions are a vast apparatus of magic, to obtain food for the tribe, and safety from the plague and the foeman. In language borrowed from the New Zealander, it is a Great TABOO.

Early man found himself in the presence of the mighty forces of nature. The thunder roared. The lightning struck his rude shelter. A hurricane ruined his crops. The fever or the foeman came upon him. He had to guess the meaning of all this. Some dead chief, much feared in life, is seen in a dream, or his ghost appears. He is silent and looks very sad. What is the cause of his sorrow? Want of food. The early savage knows no other. A storm, a pestilence vexes the clan, and the chief appears again, looking angry. The two facts are connected together. Beasts are slaughtered, and perhaps human victims, and placed near his cairn. The pestilence ceases. In this way the Hottentots have made an ancestor, Tsui Goab, into their god. Indeed, ancestor worship is the basis of all religions. But by and by, to resume our illustration, new calamities vex the tribe. Tsui Goab is angry once more. Fresh efforts are made to soothe him. Soon the Taboo develops into a number of complicated superstitions.

"The savage," says Sir John Lubbock, "is nowhere free. All over the world his daily life is regulated by a complicated, and often most inconvenient set of customs (as forcible as laws), of quaint prohibitions and privileges. . . . The Australians are governed by a code of rules and a set of customs which form one of the most cruel tyrannies that has ever, perhaps, existed on the face of the earth." ("Origin of Civilisation," p. 304.)

"The lives of savages," says Mr. Lang, "are bound by the most closely-woven fetters of custom. The simplest acts are 'tabooed.' A strict code regulates all intercourse." ("Custom and Myth.," p. 72.)

Now, unless this system is clearly understood, Mosaism will remain a riddle. It is to be observed that Ezra, far from having relaxed the reign of terror of the Great Taboo of savage survival, had enlarged the number of petty faults and superstitions; and the Levites and Pharisees at the date of Christ, far from considering all this a comedy, were the most stiff-necked of believers. It results that a new religion that proposed to ignore the chief edicts of the Taboo must have come from some strong outside influence.

The two great foes of the savage, as Mr. Frazer

shows in his able work, the "Golden Bough," were the ghost and the necromancer. The first was deemed all-powerful, and the second sought to use this power to help the tribe and injure its rivals. His art was that of the farmer, the warrior, the doctor—in fact, in his view, pure science. And the laws and ordinances were a Great Taboo, acts forbidden or enjoined to control the ghosts.

Let the Deuteronomist himself tell us what Israel was to expect if she kept these laws and ordinances.

Yahve, it is said, "will love thee, and bless thee, and multiply thee, and he will also bless the fruit of thy womb, and the fruit of thy land, thy corn, and thy wine, and thine oil, the increase of thy kine and the flocks of thy sheep. . . . The Lord will take away from thee all sickness, and will put none of the evil diseases of Egypt which thou knowest upon thee, but will lay them upon all them that hate thee. . . . Moreover, the Lord thy God will send the hornet amongst them, until they that are left, and hide themselves from thee, be destroyed."

This was the religion of Moses. The ghostly head of the clan would give abundant flocks and fertile ground to those who fed him with burnt-offerings, but failing these, would send "the blotch, the itch, the scab" (Deut. xxviii. 27), the victorious foeman—and change the fertilising rain to the "powder and dust" of the desert.

"It must be admitted that religion," says Sir John Lubbock, "as understood by the lower savage races, differs essentially from ours. Thus their deities are evil, not good. They may be forced into compliance with the wishes of man. They require bloody, and rejoice in human sacrifices. They are mortal, not immortal; a part not the author of nature. They are to be approached by dances rather than prayers, and often approve what we call vice rather than what we esteem as virtue." ("Origin of Civil," p. 133.)

In point of fact, the savage believes that sickness, death, thunder, and other human ills come not from nature, but the active interference of the god. He looks upon every one outside his tribe as an enemy. The west coast negroes represent their deities as "black and mischievous, delighting to torment them in various ways." The Bechuanas curse their deities when things go wrong. All this throws light on the god of the Hebrews. Professor Robertson Smith, in the new "Encyclopædia Britannica," describes him as immoral, but perhaps it would be more correct to say that he has the gang morality of a savage chief. He counsels the Jews to borrow the poor silver bangles of the Egyptian women, and then to treacherously carry them off (Exod. iii. 22), because gang morality recognises no rights of property outside the gang. All through the early books, stories of cheating and lying are popular.

Palestine is a narrow strip of land between the Jordan and the Mediterranean, surrounded by deserts. To it, from a city named Ur, in Chaldea, 1996 years B.C., came Abraham and the Hebrews, or "Men from Beyond." These little Semite clans were like the modern Bedouins. They did not live in towns; they pitched their tents in the country. The soil of Palestine, even in Abraham's day, was quite unable to support these teeming hordes, for the sons of Abraham went several times to Egypt to escape famine. In similar fashion, ten or twelve thousand Arabs from Tripoli and Bengazi lately left their own country to reach Egypt.

All this must be borne in mind. It has been debated whether the earliest god of Israel was a sun-god or a moon-god, and whether his name was El or Yahve. In point of fact, his name was Starvation, and the Jewish Taboo a great food-making apparatus. This accounts for the extreme ferocity with which the struggle for the land flowing with milk and honey was carried on by the rival tribes.

"When thou comest nigh to a city to fight against it, then proclaim peace to it.

"And it shall be, if it make thee an answer of peace and open unto thee, then it shall be, that all the people that is found therein shall be tributaries unto thee, and they shall serve thee.

"And if it will make no peace with thee, but will make war against thee, then thou shalt besiege it:

"And when the LORD thy God hath delivered it into thy hands, thou shalt smite every male thereof with the edge of the sword;

"But the women, and the little ones, and the cattle, and all that is in the city, even all the spoil thereof, shalt thou take unto thyself: and thou shalt eat the spoil of thine enemies, which the LORD thy God hath given thee.

"Thus shalt thou do unto all the cities which are very far off from thee, which are not of the cities of these nations."

The "cities that are very far off" mean, in reality, those that are nearer to Moses in the desert than the cities of the promised land, but the writer, composing imaginary laws for Moses in Jerusalem, some hundred years after his death, overlooked this. These are not pretty ones. These cities have to choose at once between slavery or extinction.

"But of the cities of these people, which the LORD thy God doth give thee for an inheritance, thou shalt save alive nothing that breatheth.

"But thou shalt utterly destroy them, namely the Hittites, and the Amorites, the Canaanites and the Perizzites, the Hivites and the Jebusites, as the LORD thy God hath commanded thee." (Deut. xx. 10-17.)

It accounts, too, for the ferocity of the punishments for the infringement of the Taboo. Death was the penalty. The man who fails to pour dust on the blood of a pigeon that he has knocked down with an arrow, the man who picks up sticks upon the Sabbath, the perfumer who imitates a temple smell, the man who roasts the smallest particle of fat or blood, the labourer who has an abscess and fails to take two turtle doves as a "sin offering" to the priest at "the door of the tabernacle of the congregation" (Levit. xv. 15), may all be cut off. Every one may be stoned for infringing the Taboo.

Sir John Lubbock has pointed out that the god of the savage is of limited power and intelligence, and that the Taboo was designed to control rather than conciliate him. He cites the "Eeweehs" of the Nicobar Islands, who put up scarecrows to frighten their gods, and the inhabitants of Kamtschatka, who insult their deities if their wishes are unfulfilled. He cites also the Rishis and heroes of the Indian epics, who are constantly overcoming the gods of the Indian pantheon. Certainly the early god of the Jew was not deemed all-powerful. When the Jews fought against Askelon it is recorded:—

"The LORD was with Judah, and he drove out the inhabitants of the mountain, but could not drive out the inhabitants of the valley, because they had chariots of iron." (Judges i. 19.)

He wrestles with Jacob (Gen. xxxii. 29), and the superior wrestling of the man forces the god to give his blessing. He strives to kill Moses, but fails to do it. (Exod. iv. 24.) He is a purely local god, like Kemosh and other Semitic deities.

"Surely Yahve is in this place," said Jacob in Mesopotamia, "and I knew it not."

"David himself," says M. Soury, "who was not and could not have been the monotheistic king of tradition, David, who had *teraphim* in his house, as had Jacob in his time, does he not seem to restrict the kingdom of Yahve to the land of Israel when he complains that Saul has driven him out from abiding in the inheritance of Yahve, saying, 'Go, serve other gods'? Finally, many centuries afterwards the contemporaries of Ezekiel still believed that Yahve, having abandoned the country, could no longer see them." (Ezek. ix. 9.) (Soury, "Religion of Israel," c. v.)

Anthropology divides the early races who used stone implements into two groups, the palæolithic or rough-stone-using man, and the neolithic man, who polished his implements. The editing of Ezra has burnished up the early Hebrew a little, but it is plain that he had not emerged from the stone age. His god is a stone. Jacob erected a menhir. A menhir is a piece of chipped rock, erect, huge, imposing, the neolithic man's first rude piece of sculpture, the neolithic man's god. Moses erected a circle of these stone monoliths. Joshua erected twelve stone gods on the Jordan, and sacrificed to them. (Josh. iv. 9.) Palestine abounds in such circles archæologists tell us. These circles were the "high places" of scripture.

Some hold that the Yahve who travelled with Israel in the Ark was a stone. The mighty God of Jacob is called the "Stone of Israel." (Gen. xlix. 24.) We read of Eben-ezer, the "Stone of Help," when the Ark gives the victory to Samuel. (1 Sam. vii. 12.) Daniel's "stone cut out of the mountain without hands" brake in pieces the kings and the kingdoms. (Dan. ii. 45.) The "Shem Hamphoras," the stone in the Holy of Holies in Solomon's temple, was said to be the "Stone of Jacob."

Circumcision, a savage rite, was performed with "knives of flint." (Josh. v. 2.) Mr. Tylor ("Early History of Mankind," p. 216) shows us that even at the date of the Mishna, the beast at the altar was killed with the kelt of the neolithic man. Stones were the official weights in Israel, and also the instruments of execution. David used the sling, and perhaps the chipped stone missiles that we see in museums, and his singing and dancing naked before the fetish, and the very unpleasant scalps that purchased him a wife, savour a little of the latitude of Polynesia. And his hanging up the hands and feet of Rechab and Baanah remind us of the stakes crowned with sculls round the huts of the Dyaks of Borneo.

"At a late date," says M. Soury, "we perceive in Hebrew legislation the repression of monstrous habits and depraved tastes which are only found amongst the very lowest savages. They are forbidden to tattoo themselves, to eat insects, reptiles," etc. (Levit. xi. 31; xix. 28.)

I have still to record a quaint use of stones in Israel, another survival from the stone age. In Astley's "Collection of Voyages" (vol. ii., p. 674,) it is announced that the savages of West Africa consult their god with a sort of "Odd or Even!" with nuts. In Israel, the weightiest questions were settled by the same rude divination. "The pebble is cast into the lap, but the whole disposing thereof is of the Lord." (Prov. xvi. 33.) By this odd or even Saul was chosen to be king and Jonah to be thrown overboard. By stones also malefactors were judged in the Holy of Holies, but the exact method of this is a secret that is lost.

In writing thus, of course, I do not believe myself to be dealing with the actual neolithic period. Its survivals are tough. In India before the Mutiny I was employed with a force sent to put down the rebellion of the Santals. These, a branch of the Kolárias, represent the early races that the Arya displaced. And their institutions were singularly like those of the Jews. They worshipped in "high places" rude circles of upright monoliths. They worshipped in "groves;" and on one occasion we came across a slaughtered kid still warm, that under the holy Sal tree had been sacrificed to obtain the help of Singh Bonga against us. They had, like the Jews, twelve tribes. They believed, like them, that death ended consciousness. They had marriage by capture, softened down into a comedy, like other savage tribes. They believed that all diseases were due to the wrath of evil spirits, or the spell of a sorcerer. All through the night we could hear their war tom-toms sounding, the tuph of the Jews (whence "tympanum," according to Calmet). They fought with the bows and arrows and axes that are marked "aboriginal weapons" in the South Kensington Museum. When we met them in action a chief came forward like Goliath with gestures and shouts of defiance. Like the Jews they were stiff-necked in their conservatism. Buddhism and Buddha had risen in their very midst. Brahmins, Mussulmans, Christians, had ruled them and plied them with missionaries; but pious Hindoos, instead of converting them, had been persuaded to offer sacrifices to Bagh Bhut, a tiger god, all-powerful in Santal jungles. They recited at night their deeds of theft and pillage and slaughter, like the Sioux Indians or the early Jews.

Circumcision is another savage rite. We find it with the Papuans. We find it in Central America. We find it amongst the Australian aborigines. That it was performed in Israel with knives of flint (Josh. v. 4) argues a survival from the men of stone implements. Sanitary precautions have been suggested as the origin of the rite, but such an idea would be in advance of the filthy savages using it. The "Encyclopædia Britannica" holds that it was a sacrifice to Aschera, the goddess of generation, like a somewhat similar mutilation of females. Professor Sayce ("Ancient Empires," p. 199) shows that with young men a complete mutilation in honour of the Phœnician Ashtoreth was common.

Mr. Frazer ("Golden Bough," i. 169) explains another cruel law of Leviticus. The Maoris believe that if anyone touches a dead body, and then accidentally touches food, any one partaking of that food will join the dead man in the shades. This superstition about the power of the dead is the root idea of other practices, covering pictures and looking-glasses whilst the corpse is still in the house, shunning the graveyard at night when it is buried. It is treated as an enemy who might pass his soul into the picture and do mischief. The death penalty for touching Yahve's food (Levit. vii. 21) is probably the same superstition. When God is supposed to be walking about on earth in human form, as in the instance of a semi-divine savage chief, the danger of touching his food increases enormously. Mr. Frazer shows that the Mikado used to eat every day off new rude earthenware platters, which were at once broken and buried, that no one might lose his life by accidentally touching a particle of his food. ("Golden Bough," i. 166.) Mr. Frazer gives numerous instances, where the same fatality is believed to result from food contaminated by a menstruous woman.

In the view of M. Soury, the early Jew was a

tattooed savage, who ate insects; but anthropology has shed an unexpected light on this. The families, and small clans of early savages, had each some animal as a Totem. They were tattooed with this for distinction, and it was everywhere ruled that cat could not marry cat, or fox fox. A young man tattooed as a fox would have to capture a lady with another crest, "stunning her first with a blow from his dowak" perchance, like the Australian savage discribed by Sir John Lubbock.

It has been shown by Professor Robertson Smith that the "unclean" animals of the Old Testament are these totems. "So I went in and saw, and behold every form of creeping things and abominable beasts and all the *idols of the house of Israel* pourtrayed upon the wall round about." (Ezek. viii. 10.) This accounts for the hare being "abominable" in Israel, and the beetle edible. It was meritorious to eat the totems of one's foes, but the totems of friendly tribes, and one's own totems, were tabooed. The origin of these ideas is much debated. The custom is believed to be closely connected with marriage by capture. Female infanticide was prevalent, as women only attracted ravishers. The story of the sons of Benjamin capturing the daughters of Shiloh is a frequent sort of story in savage annals. (Judges xxi.)

The sacrifice has puzzled the modern divine.

It is urged that rites are necessary to religion, and that the sacrifice was an apparatus to train Israel to a deep sense of sin, and a necessity for a blood atonement. It is contended that it was merely a form, as only the useless portions of the carcase were given to

Yahve. Those who talk like this libel the Jewish patriarchs. With savages the blood and the fat are considered the choicest morsels. To stone a poor Jew because he ate a little fat with his supper would have been infamous, if the whole affair was a harmless comedy. We have shown that the one thought of the Jew was a mighty terror, a Great Taboo. Starvation or rich harvests, victory or slavery, were due direct to Yahve; and the bloody sacrifice was the one and sole instrument by which he might be controlled.

As late as Leviticus it was believed that the burnt-offering actually provided food and drink to the Maker of the universe. It is called the "food of God" (Levit. xxi. 8), a phrase softened into "bread of God" in our version, as the "Encyclopædia Britannica" (article "Bible") has shown. It was believed also that God specially loved the smell. (Levit. viii. 21.) More important still, as pointed out by Sir John Lubbock in his "Origin of Civilisation," p. 272, human sacrifices are expressly ordered in Leviticus (xxvii. 28, 29):—

"Notwithstanding, no devoted thing that a man shall devote unto the LORD, of all that he hath, *both of man and beast*, and of the field of his possession, shall be sold or redeemed: every devoted thing is most holy unto the LORD.

"None devoted, which shall be devoted of men, shall be redeemed, but shall *surely be put to death*."

"There is indeed no doubt that human victims were offered to Yahve," says M. Soury. "The young of man belonged to Yahve, just as did the young of the animal and the fruit of the tree. All the gods of the

Semites,—El, Schaddai, Adon, Baal, Moloch, Yahve, Kemosh,—were conceived in the likeness of Eastern monarchs. They had right absolute over all that was born and all that died in their realms. Man admits his vassalage. He adores the 'master,' and brings to his lord the first-fruits of his flock, his field, and his family." ("Religion of Israel," c. vi.)

The French author goes on to say that during their sojourn in Egypt the Jews sacrificed human victims. (Ezek. xx. 26.) "In all the history of religions there is no human sacrifice better established than that of the daughter of Jephthah to Yahve. In the time of the Judges, who does not know the story of Samuel and Agag? It is 'before Yahve,' at Gilgal, that Samuel kills his victim. David appeased the wrath of Yahve, who had afflicted the land with famine during three years, by delivering up to the Gibeonites seven men of Saul's blood. The seven victims being hanged 'on the hill before Yahve,' the deity was satisfied." (2 Sam. xxi. 1-14.)

This human sacrifice is, of course, a survival of cannibalism. The Australians, as Lumholtz ("Among Cannibals," p. 70) shows, consider "talgoro" (human flesh) the daintiest of food. At their watchfires they discourse upon the delicate fat round the kidneys as an alderman might talk of calipash.

What is all this leading up to? Simply to this, that we must put far away from us the theory of modern pulpits that the bloody sacrifice was a comedy of the priest, a comedy of the Almighty. The sacrifice was not a comedy at all. To the mind of the savage it was at once business and science. It was the bank, the war office, the bureau of agriculture, the college of physicians of the nation, By it alone could the blood-loving Semite gods be influenced to give harvests, shekels, victory; and the ferocious Taboo was pure science likewise. The archer, for instance, who killed a partridge without covering the blood with earth was killed in turn, because the Taboo was a mechanism that could only be kept in working order by a remorseless attention to its most minute rules. Writers like Kuenen and Lightfoot assure us that it is quite impossible that Christianity can be due to any influence outside Judaism, because it is such a very obvious development of Jewish thought. This is a startling statement. Christianity pronounced the slaughter of animals at the altar a piece of useless folly, and tore up the great ordinances of Taboo, the Covenant between Israel and the Maker of the Heavens. It proclaimed three Gods instead of one. It pronounced that the Jewish holy books were parables rather than a statement of actual facts. Such ideas were at this epoch current in the West, owing to the activity of the missionaries of an Eastern creed.

To them we will now turn.

CHAPTER II.

Buddha.

I PROPOSE now to give a short life of Buddha, noting its points of contact with that of Jesus.

PRE-EXISTENCE IN HEAVEN.

The early Buddhists, following the example of the Vedic Brahmins, divided space into Nirvritti, the dark portion of the heavens, and Pravritti, the starry systems. Over this last, the luminous portion, Buddha figures as ruler when the legendary life opens. The Christian Gnostics took over this idea and gave to Christ a similar function. Buthos was Nirvritti ruled by "The Father" (in Buddhism by Swayambhu, the self-existent), Pravritti was the Pleroma. "It was the Father's good pleasure that in him the whole Pleroma should have its home." (Col. i. 19.)

"BEHOLD A VIRGIN SHALL CONCEIVE."

Exactly 550 years before Christ there dwelt in North Oude, at a city called Kapilavastu, the modern Nagar Khas, a king called Suddhodana. This monarch was informed by angels that a mighty teacher of men would be born miraculously in the womb of his wife. "By the consent of the king," says the "Lalita Vistara," "the queen was permitted to lead the life of a virgin for thirty-two months.' Joseph is made, a little awkwardly, to give a similar privilege to his wife. (Matt. i. 25.)

Some writers have called in question the statement that Buddha was born of a virgin, but in the southern scriptures, as given by Mr. Turnour, it is announced that a womb in which a Buddha elect has reposed, is like the sanctuary of a temple. On that account, that her womb may be sacred, the mother of a Buddha always dies in seven days. The name of the queen was borrowed from Brahminism. She was Mâyâ Devî, the Queen of Heaven. And one of the titles of this lady is Kanyâ, the Virgin of the Zodiac.

Queen Mâyâ was chosen for her mighty privilege because the Buddhist scriptures announce that the mother of a Buddha must be of royal line.

Long genealogies, very like those of the New Testament, are given also to prove the blue blood of King Suddhodana, who, like Joseph, had nothing to do with the paternity of the child. "King Mahasammata had a son named Roja, whose son was Vararoja, whose son was Kalyâna, whose son was Varakalyâna," and so on, and so on. (Dîpawanso, *see* "Journ. As. Soc.," Bengal, vol. vii., p. 925.)

How does a Buddha come down to earth? This question is debated in Heaven, and the Vedas were searched because, as Seydel shows, although Buddhism seemed a root and branch change, it was attempted to show that it was really the lofty side of the old Brahminism, a lesson not lost by and by in Palestine.

The sign of Capricorn in the old Indian Zodiac is an elephant issuing from a Makara (leviathan), and it symbolises the active god issuing from the quiescent god in his home on the face of the waters. In consequence, Buddha comes down as a white elephant, and enters the right side of the queen without piercing it or in any way injuring it. Childers sees a great analogy in all this to the Catholic theory of the perpetual virginity of Mary. Catholic doctors quote this passage from Ezekiel (xliv. 2):—

"Then said the LORD unto me, This gate shall be shut, it shall not be opened, and no man shall enter in by it; because the LORD, the God of Israel, hath entered in by it, therefore shall it be shut."

A DOUBLE ANNUNCIATION.

It is recorded that when Queen Mâyâ received the supernal Buddha in her womb, in the form of a beautiful white elephant, she said to her husband: "Like snow and silver, outshining the sun and the moon, a white elephant of six defences, with unrivalled trunk and feet, has entered my womb. Listen, I saw the three regions (earth, heaven, hell,) with a great light shining in the darkness, and myriads of spirits sang my praises in the sky."

A similar miraculous communication was made to King Suddhodana:—

"The spirits of the Pure Abode flying in the air, showed half of their forms, and hymned King Suddhodana thus:

"Guerdoned with righteousness and gentle pity,
Adored on earth and in the shining sky,
The coming Buddha quits the glorious spheres
And hies to earth to gentle Mâyâ's womb."

In the Christian scriptures there is also a double annunciation. In Luke (i. 28) the angel Gabriel is said to have appeared to the Virgin Mary before her conception, and to have foretold to her the miraculous birth of Christ. But in spite of this astounding miracle, Joseph seems to have required a second personal one before he ceased to question the chastity of his wife. (Matt. i. 19.) Plainly, two evangelists have been working the same mine independently, and a want of consistency is the result.

When Buddha was in his mother's womb that womb was transparent. The Virgin Mary was thus represented in mediæval frescoes. (*See* illustration, p. 39, in my "Buddhism in Christendom.")

"WE HAVE SEEN HIS STAR IN THE EAST."

In the Buddhist legend the devas in heaven announce that Buddha will be born when the Flower-star is seen *in the East.* (Lefman, xxi. 124; Wassiljew, p. 95.)

Amongst the thirty-two signs that indicate the mother of a Buddha, the fifth is that, like Mary the mother of Jesus, she should be "on a journey" (Beal, "Rom. History," p. 32) at the moment of parturition. This happened. A tree (palâsa, the scarlet butea) bent down its branches and overshadowed her, and Buddha came forth. Voltaire says that in the library of Berne there is a copy of the First Gospel of the Infancy, which records that a palm tree bent down in a similar manner to Mary. ("Œuvres," vol. xl.) The Koran calls it a "withered date tree."

In the First Gospel of the Infancy, it is stated that, when Christ was in His cradle, He said to His mother: "I am Jesus, the Son of God, the Word whom thou didst bring forth according to the declaration of the angel Gabriel to thee, and my Father hath sent Me for the salvation of the world."

In the Buddhist scriptures it is announced that Buddha, on seeing the light, said:—

"I am in my last birth. None is my equal. I have come to conquer death, sickness, old age. I have come to subdue the spirit of evil, and give peace and joy to the souls tormented in hell."

In the same scriptures (*see* Beal, "Rom. History," p. 46) it is announced that at the birth of the Divine child, the devas (angels) in the sky sang "their hymns and praises."

CHILD-NAMING.

"Five days after the birth of Buddha," says Bishop Bigandet, in the "Burmese Life," "was performed the ceremony of head ablution and naming the child." (P. 49.)

We see from this where the ceremony of head ablution and naming the child comes from. In the "Lalita Vistara" Buddha is carried to the temple. Plainly we have the same ceremony. There the idols bow down to him as in the First Gospel of the

Infancy the idol in Egypt bows down to Jesus. In Luke the infant Jesus is also taken to the temple by his parents to "do for him after the custom of the law." (Luke ii. 27.) What law? Certainly not the Jewish.

HEROD AND THE WISE MEN.

It is recorded in the Chinese life (Beal, "Rom. History," p. 103) that King Bimbisâra, the monarch of Râjagriha, was told by his ministers that a boy was alive for whom the stars predicted a mighty destiny. They advised him to raise an army and go and destroy this child, lest he should one day subvert the king's throne. Bimbisâra refused.

At the birth of Buddha the four Mahârâjas, the great kings, who in Hindoo astronomy guard each a cardinal point, received him. These may throw light on the traditional Persian kings that greeted Christ.

In some quarters these analogies are admitted, but it is said that the Buddhists copied from the Christian scriptures. But this question is a little complicated by the fact that many of the most noticeable similarities are in apocryphal gospels, those that were abandoned by the Church at an early date. In the Protevangelion, at Christ's birth, certain marvels are visible. The clouds are "astonished," and the birds of the air stop in their flight. The dispersed sheep of some shepherds near cease to gambol, and the shepherds to beat them. The kids near a river are arrested with their mouths close to the water. All nature seems to pause for a mighty effort. In the

"Lalita Vistara" the birds also pause in their flight when Buddha comes to the womb of Queen Mâyâ. Fires go out, and rivers are suddenly arrested in their flow.

More noticeable is the story of Asita, the Indian Simeon.

Asita dwells on Himavat, the holy mount of the Hindoos, as Simeon dwells on Mount Zion. The "Holy Ghost is upon" Simeon. That means that he has obtained the faculties of the prophet by mystical training. He "comes by the Spirit" into the temple. Asita is an ascetic, who has acquired the eight magical faculties, one of which is the faculty of visiting the Tawatinsa heavens. Happening to soar up into those pure regions one day, he is told by a host of devatas, or heavenly spirits, that a mighty Buddha is born in the world, "who will establish the supremacy of the Buddhist Dharma." The "Lalita Vistara" announces that, "looking abroad with his divine eye, and considering the kingdoms of India, he saw in the great city of Kapilavastu, in the palace of King Suddhodana, the child shining with the glitter of pure deeds, and adored by all the worlds." Afar through the skies the spirits of heaven in crowds recited the "hymn of Buddha."

This is the description of Simeon in the First Gospel of the Infancy, ii. 6—"At that time old Simeon saw Him (Christ) shining as a pillar of light when St. Mary the Virgin, His mother, carried Him in her arms, and was filled with the greatest pleasure at the sight. And the angels stood around Him, adoring Him as a King; guards stood around Him."

Asita pays a visit to the king. Asita takes the little child in his arms. Asita weeps.

"Wherefore these tears, O holy man?"

"I weep because this child will be the great Buddha, and I shall not be alive to witness the fact."

The points of contact between Simeon and Asita are very close. Both are men of God, "full of the Holy Ghost." Both are brought "by the Spirit" into the presence of the Holy Child, for the express purpose of foretelling His destiny as the Anointed One.

More remarkable still is the incident of the disputation with the doctors.

A little Brahmin was "initiated," girt with the holy thread, etc., at eight, and put under the tuition of a holy man. When Vis'vâmitra, Buddha's teacher, proposed to teach him the alphabet, the young prince went off:—

"In sounding 'A,' pronounce it as in the sound of the word 'anitya.'

"In sounding 'I,' pronounce it as in the word 'indriya.'

"In sounding 'U,' pronounce it as in the word 'upagupta.'"

And so on through the whole Sanscrit alphabet.

In the First Gospel of the Infancy, chap. xx., it is recorded that when taken to the schoolmaster Zaccheus,

"The Lord Jesus explained to him the meaning of the letters Aleph and Beth.

"8. Also, which were the straight figures of the letters, which were the oblique, and what letters had double figures; which had points and which had none; why one letter went before another; and many other things He began to tell him and explain, of which the master himself had never heard, nor read in any book.

"9. The Lord Jesus further said to the master, Take notice how I say to thee. Then He began clearly and distinctly to say Aleph, Beth, Gimel, Daleth, and so on to the end of the alphabet.

"10. At this, the master was so surprised, that he said, I believe this boy was born before Noah."

In the "Lalita Vistara" there are two separate accounts of Buddha showing his marvellous knowledge. His great display is when he competes for his wife. He then exhibits his familiarity with all lore, sacred and profane, "astronomy," the "syllogism," medicine, mystic rites.

The disputation with the doctors is considerably amplified in the twenty-first chapter of the First Gospel of the Infancy:—

"5. Then a certain principal rabbi asked Him, Hast Thou read books?

"6. Jesus answered that He had read both books and the things which were contained in books.

"7. And he explained to them the books of the law and precepts and statutes, and the mysteries which are contained in the books of the prophets—things which the mind of no creature could reach.

"8. Then said that rabbi, I never yet have seen or heard of such knowledge! What do you think that boy will be?

"9. Then a certain astronomer who was present asked the Lord Jesus whether He had studied astronomy.

"10. The Lord Jesus replied, and told him the number of the spheres and heavenly bodies, as also their triangular, square, and sextile aspects, their progressive and retrogade motions, their size and several prognostications, and other things which the reason of man had never discovered.

"11. There was also among them a philosopher, well skilled in physic and natural philosophy, who asked the Lord Jesus whether He had studied physic.

"12. He replied, and explained to him physics and metaphysics.

"13. Also those things which were above and below the power of nature.

"14. The powers also of the body, its humours and their effects.

"15. Also the number of its bones, veins, arteries, and nerves.

"16. The several constitutions of body, hot and dry, cold and moist, and the tendencies of them.

"17. How the soul operated on the body.

"18. What its various sensations and faculties were.

"19. The faculty of speaking, anger, desire.

"20. And, lastly, the manner of its composition and dissolution, and other things which the understanding of no creature had ever reached.

"21. Then that philosopher worshipped the Lord Jesus, and said, O Lord Jesus, from henceforth I will be Thy disciple and servant."

Vis'vâmitra in like manner worshipped Buddha by falling at his feet.

THE MYSTERIES OF THE KINGDOM OF HEAVEN.

I have now come to a stage in this narrative when a few remarks are necessary. The "Lalita Vistara" professes to reveal the secrets of the Buddhas, the secrets of "magic," the secrets of Yoga, or union with Brahma. And whether it be fiction or history, it does so more roundly than any other work. The Christian gospels profess also to teach a similar secret. Read by the light of the Buddhist book, I think they do teach it. But read alone, eighteen centuries come forward to show that they do not.

The highest spiritual philosophers in Buddhism, in Brahminism, in Christendom, in Islam, announce two kingdoms distinct from one another. They are called in India the Domain of Appetite (Kâmaloca), and the Domain of Spirit (Brahmaloca). The "Lalita Vistara" throughout describes a conflict between these two great camps. Buddha is offered a crown by his father. He has wives, palaces, jewels, but he leaves all for the thorny jungle where the Brahmacharin dreamt his dreams of God. This is called pessimism by some writers, who urge that we should enjoy life as we find it, but modern Europe having tried, denies that life is so enjoyable. Its motto is *Tout lasse, tout casse, tout passe.* Yes, say the optimists, but we needn't all live a life like Jay Gould. A good son, a good father, a good husband, a good citizen, is happy enough. True, reply the pessimists, in so far as a mortal enters the domain of spirit he may be happy, for that is not a region but a state of the mind. But mundane accidents seem, almost by rule, to mar even that happiness. The husband loses his loved one, the artist his eyesight. Philosophers and statesmen find their great dreams and schemes baffled by the infirmities of age.

Age, disease, death! These are the evils for which the great Indian allegory proposes to find a remedy. Let us see what that remedy is.

CHAPTER III.

The Four Presaging Tokens.

SOOTHSAYERS were consulted by King Suddhodana. They pronounced the following:—

"The young boy will, without doubt, be either a king of kings, or a great Buddha. If he is destined to be a great Buddha, four presaging tokens will make his mission plain. He will see—

"1. An old man.

"2. A sick man.

"3. A corpse.

"4. A holy recluse.

"If he fails to see these four presaging tokens of an avatâra, he will be simply a Chakravartin" (king of earthly kings).

King Suddhodana, who was a trifle worldly, was very much comforted by the last prediction of the soothsayers. He thought in his heart, It will be an easy thing to keep these four presaging tokens from the young prince. So he gave orders that three magnificent palaces should at once be built—the Palace of Spring, the Palace of Summer, the Palace of Winter. These palaces, as we learn from the "Lalita Vistara," were the most beautiful palaces ever conceived on earth. Indeed, they were quite able to cope in splendour with Vaijayanta, the immortal palace of

Indra himself. Costly pavilions were built out in all directions, with ornamented porticoes and burnished doors. Turrets and pinnacles soared into the sky. Dainty little windows gave light to the rich apartments. Galleries, balustrades, and delicate trellis-work were abundant everywhere. A thousand bells tinkled on each roof. We seem to have the lacquered Chinese edifices of the pattern which architects believe to have flourished in early India. The gardens of these fine palaces rivalled the chess-board in the rectangular exactitude of their parterres and trellis-work bowers. Cool lakes nursed on their calm bosoms storks and cranes, wild geese and tame swans; ducks, also, as parti-coloured as the white, red, and blue lotuses amongst which they swam. Bending to these lakes were bowery trees—the champak, the acacia serisha, and the beautiful asoka tree with its orange-scarlet flowers. Above rustled the mimosa, the fan-palm, and the feathery pippala, Buddha's tree. The air was heavy with the strong scent of the tuberose and the Arabian jasmine.

It must be mentioned that strong ramparts were prepared round the palaces of Kapilavastu, to keep out all old men, sick men, and recluses, and, I must add, to keep in the prince.

And a more potent safeguard still was designed. When the prince was old enough to marry, his palace was deluged with beautiful women. He revelled in the "five dusts," as the Chinese version puts it. But a shock was preparing for King Suddhodana.

This is how the matter came about. The king had prepared a garden even more beautiful than the garden of the Palace of Summer. A soothsayer had told him that if he could succeed in showing the prince this garden, the prince would be content to remain in it with his wives for ever. No task seemed easier than this, so it was arranged that on a certain day the prince should be driven thither in his chariot. But, of course, immense precautions had to be taken to keep all old men and sick men and corpses from his sight. Quite an army of soldiers were told off for this duty, and the city was decked with flags. The path of the prince was strewn with flowers and scents, and adorned with vases of the rich kadali plant. Above were costly hangings and garlands, and pagodas of bells.

But, lo and behold! as the prince was driving along, plump under the wheels of his chariot, and before the very noses of the silken nobles and the warriors with javelins and shields, he saw an unusual sight. This was an old man, very decrepit and very broken. The veins and nerves of his body were swollen and prominent; his teeth chattered; he was wrinkled, bald, and his few remaining hairs were of dazzling whiteness; he was bent very nearly double, and tottered feebly along, supported by a stick.

"What is this, O coachman?" said the prince. "A man with his blood all dried up, and his muscles glued to his body! His head is white; his teeth knock together; he is scarcely able to move along, even with the aid of that stick!"

"Prince," said the coachman, "this is Old Age. This man's senses are dulled; suffering has destroyed his spirit; he is contemned by his neighbours. Unable to help himself, he has been abandoned in this forest."

"Is this a peculiarity of his family?" demanded the prince, "or is it the law of the world? Tell me quickly."

"Prince," said the coachman, "it is neither a law of his family, nor a law of the kingdom. In every being youth is conquered by age. Your own father and mother and all your relations will end in old age. There is no other issue to humanity."

"Then youth is blind and ignorant," said the prince, "and sees not the future. If this body is to be the abode of old age, what have I to do with pleasure and its intoxications? Turn round the chariot, and drive me back to the palace!"

Consternation was in the minds of all the courtiers at this untoward occurrence; but the odd circumstance of all was that no one was ever able to bring to condign punishment the miserable author of the mischief. The old man could never be found.

King Suddhodana was at first quite beside himself with tribulation. Soldiers were summoned from the distant provinces, and a cordon of detachments thrown out to a distance of four miles in each direction, to keep the other presaging tokens from the prince. By and by the king became a little more quieted. A ridiculous accident had interfered with his plans: "If my son could see the Garden of Happiness he never would become a hermit." The king determined that another attempt should be made. But this time the precautions were doubled.

On the first occasion the prince left the Palace of

Summer by the eastern gate. The second expedition was through the southern gate.

But another untoward event occurred. As the prince was driving along in his chariot, suddenly he saw close to him a man emaciated, ill, loathsome, burning with fever. Companionless, uncared for, he tottered along, breathing with extreme difficulty.

"Coachman," said the prince, "what is this man, livid and loathsome in body, whose senses are dulled, and whose limbs are withered? His stomach is oppressing him; he is covered with filth. Scarcely can he draw the breath of life!"

"Prince," said the coachman, "this is Sickness. This poor man is attacked with a grievous malady. Strength and comfort have shunned him. He is friendless, hopeless, without a country, without an asylum. The fear of death is before his eyes."

"If the health of man," said Buddha, "is but the sport of a dream, and the fear of coming evils can put on so loathsome a shape, how can the wise man, who has seen what life really means, indulge in its vain delights? Turn back, coachman, and drive me to the palace!"

The angry king, when he heard what had occurred, gave orders that the sick man should be seized and punished, but although a price was placed on his head, and he was searched for far and wide, he could never be caught. A clue to this is furnished by a passage in the "Lalita Vistara." The sick man was in reality one of the Spirits of the Pure Abode, masquerading in sores and spasms. These Spirits of the Pure Abode are also called the Buddhas of the Past, in many passages. The answers of the coachman were due to their inspiration.

It would almost seem as if some influence, malefic or otherwise, was stirring the good King Suddhodana. Unmoved by failure, he urged the prince to a third effort. The chariot this time was to set out by the western gate. Greater precautions than ever were adopted. The chain of guards was posted at least twelve miles off from the Palace of Summer. But the Buddhas of the Past again arrested the prince. His chariot was suddenly crossed by a phantom funeral procession. A phantom corpse, smeared with the orthodox mud, and spread with a sheet, was carried on a bier. Phantom women wailed, and phantom musicians played on the drum and the Indian flute. No doubt also, phantom Brahmins chanted hymns to Jatavedas, to bear away the immortal part of the dead man to the home of the Pitris.

"What is this?" said the prince. "Why do these women beat their breast and tear their hair? Why do these good folks cover their heads with the dust of the ground? And that strange form upon its litter, wherefore is it so rigid?"

"Prince," said the charioteer, "this is Death! Yon form, pale and stiffened, can never again walk and move. Its owner has gone to the unknown caverns of Yama. His father, his mother, his child, his wife cry out to him, but he cannot hear."

Buddha was sad.

"Woe be to youth, which is the sport of age! Woe be to health, which is the sport of many maladies! Woe be to life, which is as a breath! Woe be to the idle pleasures which debauch humanity! But for the 'five aggregations' there would be no age, sickness, nor death. Go back to the city. I must compass the deliverance."

A fourth time the prince was urged by his father to visit the Garden of Happiness. The chain of guards this time was sixteen miles away. The exit was by the northern gate. But suddenly a calm man of gentle mien, wearing an ochre-red cowl, was seen in the roadway.

"Who is this," said the prince, "rapt, gentle, peaceful in mien? He looks as if his mind were far away elsewhere. He carries a bowl in his hand."

"Prince, this is the New Life," said the charioteer. "That man is of those whose thoughts are fixed on the eternal Brahma [Brahmacharin]. He seeks the divine voice. He seeks the divine vision. He carries the alms-bowl of the holy beggar [bhikshu]. His mind is calm, because the gross lures of the lower life can vex it no more."

"Such a life I covet," said the prince. "The lusts of man are like the sea-water—they mock man's thirst instead of quenching it. I will seek the divine vision, and give immortality to man!"

King Suddhodana was beside himself. He placed five hundred corseleted Sakyas at every gate of the Palace of Summer. Chains of sentries were round the walls, which were raised and strengthened. A phalanx of loving wives, armed with javelins, was posted round the prince's bed to "narrowly watch" him. The king ordered also all the allurements of sense to be constantly presented to the prince.

"Let the women of the zenana cease not for an instant their concerts and mirth and sports. Let them shine in silks and sparkle in diamonds and emeralds."

The allegory is in reality a great battle between two camps—the denizens of the Kâmaloca, or the Domains of Appetite, and the denizens of the Brahmaloca, the Domains of Pure Spirit. The latter are unseen, but not unfelt.

For one day, when the prince reclined on a silken couch listening to the sweet crooning of four or five brown-skinned, large-eyed Indian girls, his eyes suddenly assumed a dazed and absorbed look, and the rich hangings and garlands and intricate trellis-work of the golden apartment were still present, but dim to his mind. And music and voices, more sweet than he had ever listened to, seemed faintly to reach him. I will write down some of the verses.

"Mighty prop of humanity
March in the pathway of the Rishis of old,
Go forth from this city!
Upon this desolate earth,
When thou hast acquired the priceless knowledge of the Jinas,
When thou hast become a perfect Buddha,
Give to all flesh the baptism (river) of the kingdom of Righteousness,
Thou who once didst sacrifice thy feet, thy hands, thy precious body, and all thy riches for the world,
Thou whose life is pure, save flesh from its miseries!
In the presence of reviling be patient, O conqueror of self!
Lord of those who possess two feet, go forth on thy mission!
Conquer the evil one and his army."

In the end the Buddhas of the Past triumph. They

persuade Buddha to flee away from his cloying pleasures and become a Yogi.

"THEN WAS JESUS LED UP BY THE SPIRIT INTO THE WILDERNESS, TO BE TEMPTED OF THE DEVIL."

Comfortable dowagers driving to church three times on Sunday would be astonished to learn that the essence of Christianity is in this passage. Its meaning has quite passed away from Protestantism, almost from Christendom. The "Lalita Vistara" fully shows what that meaning is. Without Buddhism it would be lost. Jesus was an Essene, and the Essene, like the Indian Yogi, sought to obtain divine union and the "gifts of the Spirit" by solitary reverie in retired spots. In what is called the "Monastery of our Lord" on the Quarantania, a cell is shown with rude frescoes of Jesus and Satan. There, according to tradition, the demoniac hauntings that all mystics speak of occurred.

"I HAVE NEED TO BE BAPTISED OF THEE."

A novice in Yoga has a guru, or teacher. Buddha, in riding away from the palace by and by reached a jungle near Vaisalî. He at once put himself under a Brahmin Yogi named Arâta Kâlâma, but his spiritual insight developed so rapidly that in a short time the Yogi offered to Buddha, the arghya, the offering of rice, flowers, sesamun, etc., that the humble novice usually presents to his instructor, and asked him to teach instead of learning. (Foucaux, "Lalita Vistara," p. 228.)

THIRTY YEARS OF AGE.

M. Ernest de Bunsen, in his work, "The Angel Messiah," says that Buddha, like Christ, commenced preaching at thirty years of age. He certainly must have preached at Vaisalî, for five young men became his disciples there, and exhorted him to go on with his teaching. ("Lalita Vistara," p. 236.) He was twenty-nine when he left the palace, therefore he might well have preached at thirty. He did not turn the wheel of the law until after a six years' meditation under the Tree of Knowledge.

BAPTISM.

The Buddhist rite of baptism finds its sanction in two incidents in the Buddhist scriptures. In the first, Buddha bathes in the holy river, and Mâra, the evil spirit, tries to prevent him from emerging. In the second, angels administer the holy rite (Abhisheka).

"AND WHEN HE HAD FASTED FORTY DAYS AND FORTY NIGHTS."

Buddha, immediately previous to his great encounter with Mâra, the tempter, fasted forty-nine days and nights. ("Chinese Life," by Wung Puh.)

"COMMAND THAT THESE STONES BE MADE BREAD."

The first temptation of Buddha, when Mâra assailed

him under the bo tree, is precisely similar to that of Jesus. His long fast had very nearly killed him. "Sweet creature, you are at the point of death. Sacrifice food." This meant, eat a portion to save your life.

"AGAIN THE DEVIL TAKETH HIM UP INTO AN EXCEEDING HIGH MOUNTAIN," ETC.

The second temptation of Mâra is also like one of Satan's. The tempter, by a miracle, shows Buddha the glorious city of Kapilavastu, twisting the earth round like the "wheel of a potter" to do this. He offers to make him a mighty king of kings (Chakravartin) in seven days. (Bigandet, p. 65.)

THE THIRD TEMPTATION.

Jewish prudery has quite marred the third temptation. From the days of Krishna and the phantom naked woman, Kotavî, to the days of St. Anthony and St. Jerome, or even to the days of mediæval monasteries with their incubi and succubi, sex temptations have been a prominent feature of the fasting ascetic's visions. The daughters of Mâra, the tempter, in exquisite forms, now come round Buddha. In the end he converts these pretty ladies, and converts and baptises Mâra himself.

"AND ANGELS CAME AND MINISTERED UNTO HIM."

After his conflict with Mâra, angels come to greet him.

"GLAD TIDINGS OF GREAT JOY."

Buddha, on vanquishing Mâra, left Buddha Gaya for the deer forest of Benares. There he began to preach. His doctrine is called Subha Shita (glad tidings). (*See* Rajendra L. Mitra "N. Buddhist Lit.," p. 29.)

"BEHOLD A GLUTTONOUS PERSON!"

Five disciples who left him when he gave over the rigid fasts of the Brahmins, called out on seeing him in the deer forest, "Behold a gluttonous person!" (*relaché et gourmand*).

"FOLLOW ME."

Almost his first converts were thirty profligate young men, whom he met sporting with lemans in the Kappasya jungle. "He received them," says Professor Rhys Davids, "into the order, with the formula, 'Follow Me.'" ("Birth Stories," p. 114.)

THE TWELVE GREAT DISCIPLES.

"Except in my religion, the twelve great disciples are not to be found." (Bigandet, p. 301.)

"THE DISCIPLE WHOM JESUS LOVED."

One disciple was called Upatishya (the beloved disciple). In a former existence, he and Maudgalyâyana had prayed that they might sit, the one on the right hand and the other on the left. Buddha granted this prayer. The other disciples murmured much. (Bigandet, p. 153.)

"GO YE INTO ALL THE WORLD."

From Benares Buddha sent forth the sixty-one disciples. "Go ye forth," he said, "and preach Dharma, no two disciples going the same way." (Bigandet, p. 126.)

"THE SAME CAME TO JESUS BY NIGHT."

Professor Rhys Davids points out that Yâsas, a young rich man, came to Buddha by night for fear of his rich relations.

PAX VOBISCUM.

On one point I have been a little puzzled. The password of the Buddhist Wanderers was Sadhu! which does not seem to correspond with the "Pax Vobiscum!" (Matt. x. 13) of Christ's disciples. But I have just come across a passage in Renan ("Les Apôtres," p. 22) which shows that the Hebrew word was Schalom! (*bonheur!*) This is almost a literal translation of Sadhu!

Burnouf says that by preaching and miracle Buddha's religion was established. In point of fact it was the first universal religion. He invented the preacher and the missionary.

"A NEW COMMANDMENT GIVE I YOU, THAT YE LOVE ONE ANOTHER."

"By love alone can we conquer wrath. By good

alone can we conquer evil. The whole world dreads violence. All men tremble in the presence of death. Do to others that which ye would have them do to you. Kill not. Cause no death." ("Sûtra of Forty-two Sections," v. 129.)

"Say no harsh words to thy neighbour. He will reply to thee in the same tone." (*Ibid.* v. 133.)

"'I am injured and provoked, I have been beaten and plundered!' They who speak thus will never cease to hate." (*Ibid.* v. 4, 5.)

"That which can cause hate to cease in the world is not hate, but the absence of hate."

"If, like a trumpet trodden on in battle, thou complainest not, thou has attained Nirvâna."

"Silently shall I endure abuse, as the war-elephant receives the shaft of the bowman."

"The awakened man goes not on revenge, but rewards with kindness the very being who has injured him, as the sandal tree scents the axe of the woodman who fells it."

THE BEATITUDES.

The Buddhists, like the Christians, have got their Beatitudes. They are plainly arranged for chant and response in the temples. It is to be noted that the Christian Beatitudes were a portion of the early Christian ritual.

"*An Angel.*

"1 Many angels and men
Have held various things blessings.
When they were yearning for the inner wisdom.
Do thou declare to us the chief good.

"*Buddha.*

"2 Not to serve the foolish,
But to serve the spiritual;
To honour those worthy of honour,—
This is the greatest blessing.

"3 To dwell in a spot that befits one's condition,
To think of the effect of one's deeds,
To guide the behaviour aright,—
This is the greatest blessing.

"4 Much insight and education,
Self-control and pleasant speech,
And whatever word be well spoken,—
This is the greatest blessing.

"5 To support father and mother,
To cherish wife and child,
To *follow a peaceful calling*,—
This is the greatest blessing.

"6 To *bestow alms* and *live righteously*
To give help to kindred,
Deeds which cannot be blamed,—
These are the greatest blessing.

"7 To *abhor and cease from sin*,
Abstinence from strong drink,
Not to be weary in well-doing,—
These are the greatest blessing.

"8 *Reverence* and lowliness,
Contentment and gratitude,
The hearing of Dharma at due seasons,—
This is the greatest blessing.

"9 To be *long-suffering* and *meek*,
To associate with the tranquil,
Religious talk at due seasons,—
This is the greatest blessing.

"10 *Self-restraint* and *purity*,
The knowledge of noble truths,
The attainment of Nirvâna,—
This is the greatest blessing.

THE ONE THING NEEDFUL.

Certain subtle questions were proposed to Buddha, such as: What will best conquer the evil passions of man? What is the most savoury gift for the alms-bowl of the mendicant? Where is true happiness to be found? Buddha replied to them all with one word, *Dharma* (the heavenly life). (Bigandet, p. 225.)

"WHOSOEVER SHALL SMITE THEE ON THY RIGHT CHEEK OFFER HIM THE OTHER ALSO."

A merchant from Sûnaparanta having joined Buddha's society, was desirous of preaching to his relations, and is said to have asked the permission of the master so to do.

"The people of Sûnaparanta," said Buddha, "are exceedingly violent; if they revile you what will you do?"

"I will make no reply," said the mendicant.

"And if they strike you?"

"I will not strike in return," said the mendicant.

"And if they kill you?"

"Death," said the missionary, "is no evil in itself. Many even desire it to escape from the vanities of life." (Bigandet, p. 216.)

BUDDHA'S THIRD COMMANDMENT.

"Commit no adultery." Commentary by Buddha: "This law is broken by even looking at the wife of another with a lustful mind." (Buddhaghosa's "Parables," by Max Müller and Rogers, p. 153.)

THE SOWER.

It is recorded that Buddha once stood beside the ploughman Kasibhâradvaja, who reproved him for his idleness. Buddha answered thus:—"I, too, plough and sow, and from my ploughing and sowing I reap immortal fruit. My field is religion. The weeds that I pluck up are the passions of cleaving to this life. My plough is wisdom, my seed purity." ("Hardy Manual," p. 215.)

On another occasion he described almsgiving as being like "good seed sown on a good soil that yields an abundance of fruits. But alms given to those who are yet under the tyrannical yoke of the passions, are like a seed deposited in a bad soil. The passions of the receiver of the alms, choke, as it were, the growth of merits." (Bigandet, p. 211.)

"NOT THAT WHICH GOETH INTO THE MOUTH DEFILETH A MAN."

In the "Sutta Nipâta," chap. ii., is a discourse on the food that defiles a man (Âmaghanda). Therein it is explained at some length that the food that is eaten cannot defile a man, but "destroying living beings, killing, cutting, binding, stealing, falsehood, adultery, evil thoughts, murder,"—this defiles a man, not the eating of flesh.

"WHERE YOUR TREASURE IS."

"A man," says Buddha, "buries a treasure in a deep pit, which lying concealed therein day after day profits him nothing, but there is a treasure of charity, piety, temperance, soberness, a treasure secure, impregnable, that cannot pass away, a treasure that no thief can steal. Let the wise man practise Dharma. This is a treasure that follows him after death." ("Khuddaka Pâtha," p. 13.)

THE HOUSE ON THE SAND.

"It [the seen world] is like a city of sand. Its foundation cannot endure." ("Lalita Vistara," p. 172.)

BLIND GUIDES.

"Who is not freed cannot free others. The blind cannot guide in the way." (*Ibid.* p. 179.)

"AS YE SOW, SO SHALL YE REAP."

"As men sow, thus shall they reap." ("Ta-chwang-yan-king-lun," sermon 57.)

"A CUP OF COLD WATER TO ONE OF THESE LITTLE ONES."

"Whosoever piously bestows a little water shall receive an ocean in return." ("Ta-chwang-yan-king-lun," sermon 20).

"BE NOT WEARY IN WELL-DOING."

"Not to be weary in well-doing." ("Mahâmangala Sutta," ver. 7.)

"GIVE TO HIM THAT ASKETH."

"Give to him that asketh, even though it be but a little." ("Udânavarga," ch. xx. ver. 15.)

"DO UNTO OTHERS," ETC.

"With pure thoughts and fulness of love I will do towards others what I do for myself." ("Lalita Vistara," ch. v.)

"PREPARE YE THE WAY OF THE LORD!"

"Buddha's triumphant entry into Râjagriha (the "City of the King") has been compared to Christ's entry into Jerusalem. Both, probably, never occurred, and only symbolise the advent of a divine Being to earth. It is recorded in the Buddhist scriptures that on these occasions a "Precursor of Buddha" always appears. (Bigandet, p. 147.)

"WHO DID SIN, THIS MAN OR HIS PARENTS, THAT HE WAS BORN BLIND?" (John ix. 3.)

Professor Kellogg, in his work entitled "The Light of Asia and the Light of the World," condemns Buddhism in nearly all its tenets. But he is especially emphatic in the matter of the metempsychosis. The poor and hopeless Buddhist has to begin again and again "the weary round of birth and death," whilst the righteous Christians go at once into life eternal.

Now it seems to me that this is an example of the danger of contrasting two historical characters when we have a strong sympathy for the one and a strong prejudice against the other. Professor Kellogg has conjured up a Jesus with nineteenth century ideas, and a Buddha who is made responsible for all the fancies that were in the world B.C. 500. Professor Kellogg is a professor of an American university, and as such must know that the doctrine of the *gilgal* (the Jewish name for the metempsychosis) was as universal in Palestine A.D. 30, as it was in Râjagriha B.C. 500. An able writer in the *Church Quarterly Review* of October, 1885, maintains that the Jews brought it from Babylon. Dr. Ginsburg, in his work on the "Kabbalah," shows that the doctrine continued to be held by Jews as late as the ninth century of our era. He shows, too, that St. Jerome has recorded that it was "propounded amongst the early Christians as an esoteric and traditional doctrine."

The author of the article in the *Church Quarterly*

Review, in proof of its existence, adduces the question put by the disciples of Christ in reference to the man that was born blind. And if it was considered that a man could be born blind as a punishment for sin, that sin must have been plainly committed before his birth. Oddly enough, in the "White Lotus of Dharma" there is an account of the healing of a blind man, "Because of the sinful conduct of the man [in a former birth] this malady has risen."

But a still more striking instance is given in the case of the man sick with the palsy. (Luke v. 18.) The Jews believed, with modern Orientals, that grave diseases like paralysis were due, not to physical causes in this life, but to moral causes in previous lives. And if the account of the cure of the paralytic is to be considered historical, it is quite clear that this was Christ's idea when He cured the man, for He distinctly announced that the cure was affected not by any physical processes, but by annulling the "sins" which were the cause of his malady.

Traces of the metempsychosis idea still exist in Catholic Christianity. The doctrine of original sin is said by some writers to be a modification of it. Certainly the fancy that the works of supererogation of their saints can be transferred to others is the Buddhist idea of good karma, which is transferable in a similar manner.

"IF THE BLIND LEAD THE BLIND, BOTH SHALL FALL INTO THE DITCH." (Matt. xv. 14.)

"As when a string of blind men are clinging one to

the other, neither can the foremost see, nor the middle one see, nor the hindmost see. Just so, methinks, Vâsittha is the talk of the Brahmins versed in the Three Vedas." (Buddha, in the "Tevigga Sutta," i. 15.)

"EUNUCHS FOR THE KINGDOM OF HEAVEN'S SAKE."

In the days of St. Thomas à Kempis the worshipper was modelled on the Christ. In our days, the Christ seems modelled on the worshipper. The Bodleian professor of Sanscrit writes thus: "Christianity teaches that in the highest form of life love is intensified. Buddhism teaches that in the highest state of existence all love is extinguished. According to Christianity—Go and earn your own bread and support yourself and your family. Marriage, it says, is honourable and undefiled, and married life a field where holiness can grow."

But history is history; and a French writer has recently attacked Christ for attempting to bring into Europe the celibacy and pessimism of Buddhism. This author in his work, "Jésus Bouddha," cites Luke xiv. 26:—

"If any man come to Me, and hate not his father, and mother, and *wife*, and children, and brethren, and sisters, yea, and his own life also, he cannot be My disciple."

He adduces also:—

"Let the dead bury their dead."

"Think not that I have come to send peace on earth: I come not to send peace, but a sword. For I am come to set a man at variance against his father, and the daughter against her mother, and the daughter-in-law against her mother-in-law. And a man's foes shall be they of his own household." (Matt. x. 34-36.)

"And the brother shall deliver up the brother to death, and the father the child; and the children shall rise up against their parents, and cause them to be put to death." (*Ibid.* ver. 21.)

"So likewise, whosoever he be of you that forsaketh not all that he hath, he cannot be my disciple." (Luke xiv. 33).

The author says that all this is pure nihilism, and Essene communism. "The most sacred family ties are to be renounced, and man to lose his individuality and become a unit in a vast scheme to overturn the institutions of his country."

"Qu' importe au fanatisme la ruine de la societé humaine."

"The anticosmic tendency of the Christian doctrine," says Mr. Felix Oswald ("Secret of the East," p. 27), "distinguishes it from all religions except Buddhism. In the language of the New Testament the 'world' is everywhere a synonym of evil and sin, the flesh everywhere the enemy of the spirit. . . . The Gospel of Buddha, though a pernicious, is, however, a perfectly consistent doctrine. Birth, life, and re-birth is an eternal round of sorrow and disappointment. The present and the future are but the upper and lower tire of an ever-rolling wheel of woe. The only salvation from the wheel of life is an escape to the peace of Nirvâna. The attempt to graft this doctrine upon the optimistic theism of Palestine has made the

Christian ethics inconsistent and contradictory. A paternal Jehovah who yet eternally and horribly tortures a vast plurality of his children. An earth the perfect work of a benevolent God, yet a vale of tears not made to be enjoyed, but only to be despised and renounced. An omnipotent heaven, and yet unable to prevent the intrigues and constant victories of hell. Christianity is evidently not a homogeneous but a composite, a hybrid religion; and considered in connection with the indications of history, and the evidence of the above-named ethical and traditional analogies, these facts leave no reasonable doubt that the founder of the Galilean Church was a disciple of Buddha Sakya muni." (P. 139.)

All this is very well if the Buddhists by "salvation" meant escape from life, and not from sin. A "pessimist" Buddhist kingdom, according to this, ought to present the universal sad faces of the "Camelot" of a modern school of artists, and yet the Burmese are pronounced by all to be the merriest and happiest of God's creatures. We know, too, that India never was so prosperous as in the days of Buddhist rule. The monks carried agriculture to high perfection; and Indian fabrics were famous everywhere. A convent meant less a career than an education in spiritual knowledge. Like the Essene, the Buddhist monk was not forced to remain for life. Catholicism introduced that change.

"THEN ALL HIS DISCIPLES FORSOOK HIM AND FLED."

It is recorded that on one occasion when a "must"

elephant charged furiously, "all the disciples deserted Buddha. Ananda alone remained." ("Fo-sho-hing-tsan-king," iv. 21.)

"IF THY RIGHT EYE OFFEND THEE."

Mr. Felix Oswald ("The Secret of the East," p. 134) announces, without however giving a more detailed reference, that according to Max Muller's translation of the "Ocean of Worlds," a young monk meets a rich woman who pities his hard lot.

"Blessed is the woman who looks into thy lovely eyes!"

"Lovely!" replied the monk. "Look here!" And plucking out one of his eyes he held it up, bleeding and ghastly, and asked her to correct her opinion.

WALKING ON THE WATER.

Certain villagers, hard of belief, were listening to Buddha on the shore of a mighty river. Suddenly by a miracle the great teacher caused a man to appear walking on the water from the other side, without immersing his feet. ("Chinese Dhammapada," p. 51.)

"AND LO! THERE WAS A GREAT CALM."

Pûrna, one of Buddha's disciples, had a brother in danger of shipwreck in a "black storm." But the guardian spirits of Pûrna informed him of this. He at once transported himself through the air from the distant inland town to the deck of the ship. "Immediately the black tempest ceased as if Sumeru had arrested it." (Burnouf, Introd., p. 229.)

A BUDDHA MULTIPLYING FOOD.

Buddha once narrated a story of a former Buddha, who visited King Sudarsana in his city of Jambunada (Fu-pen-hing-tsi-king).

Now in that city was a man who was the next day to be married, and he much wished the Buddha to come to the feast. Buddha, passing by, read his silent wish, and consented to come. The bridegroom was overjoyed, and scattered many flowers over his house and sprinkled it with perfumes.

The next day Buddha with his alms-bowl in his hand and with a retinue of many followers arrived; and when they had taken their seats in due order, the host distributed every kind of exquisite food, saying, "Eat, my lord, and all the congregation, according to your desire."

But now a marvel presented itself to the astonished mind of the host. Although all these holy men ate very heartily, the meats and the drinks remained positively quite undiminished; whereupon he argued in his mind, "If I could only invite all my kinsmen to come, the banquet would be sufficient for them likewise."

And now another marvel was presented. Buddha read the good man's thought, and all the relatives without invitation streamed in at the door. They, also, fed heartily on the miraculous food.

"WHY EATETH YOUR MASTER WITH PUBLICANS AND SINNERS?" (Matt. ix. 10.)

The Courtesan Amrapalî invited Buddha and his disciples to a banquet in the mango grove at Vaisalî. Buddha accepted. Some rich princes, sparkling in emeralds, came and gave him a similar invitation He refused. They were very angry to see him sit at meat with Amrapalî. He explained to his disciples that the harlot might enter the kingdom of Dharma more easily than the prince. (Bigandet, p. 251.)

THE PENITENT THIEF.

Buddha confronts a terrible bandit in his mountain retreat and converts him. ("Chinese Dhammapada," p. 98.)

"THERE WAS WAR IN HEAVEN."

Professor Beal, in his "Catena of Buddhist Scriptures" (p. 52), tells us that, in the "Saddharma Prâkasa Sasana Sûtra," a great war in heaven is described. In it the "wicked dragons" assault the legions of heaven. After a terrific conflict they are driven down by Indra and the heavenly hosts.

"THE KINGDOM OF HEAVEN IS LIKE UNTO A MERCHANTMAN SEEKING GOODLY PEARLS, WHO, WHEN HE HAD FOUND ONE PEARL OF GREAT PRICE, WENT AND SOLD ALL THAT HE HAD AND BOUGHT IT." (Matt. xiii. 45.)

The most sacred emblem of Buddhism is called the

mani (pearl), and in the Chinese biography, a merchant-man seeking goodly pearls finds it, and unfortunately drops it into the sea. Rather than lose it he tries to drain the sea dry. ("Rom. Hist.," p. 228.)

THE VOICE FROM THE SKY.

This sounds often in the Buddhist narratives. (*See* Beal, "Rom. Hist.," p. 105.)

FAITH.

"Faith is the first gate of the Law." ("Lalita Vistara," p. 39.)

"All who have faith in me obtain a mighty joy." (*Ibid.* p. 188.)

"THOU ART NOT YET FIFTY YEARS OLD, AND HAST THOU SEEN ABRAHAM?"

In the "White Lotus of Dharma" (ch. xiv.) Buddha is asked how it is that having sat under the bo tree only forty years ago he has been able, according to his boast, to see many Buddhas and saints who died hundreds of years previously. He answers that he has lived many hundred thousand myriads of Kotis, and that though in the form of a Buddha, he is in reality Swayambhu, the Self-Existent, the Father of the million worlds. In proof of this statement, he causes two Buddhas of the Past, Prabhûtaratna and Gadgadesvara, to appear in the sky. The first pronounces loudly these words: "It is well! It is well!"

These Buddhas appear with their sepulchral canopies (stupas) of diamonds, red pearls, emeralds, etc. Peter, at the scene of the Transfiguration, said to Christ:—

"Let us make here three tabernacles, one for Thee, one for Moses, and one for Elias." Why should Peter want to adopt a Buddhist custom and build tabernacles for the dead Moses and the dead Elias? Why, also, should Moses come from the tomb to support a teacher who had torn his covenant with Yahve to shreds?

"HE WAS TRANSFIGURED BEFORE THEM."

Buddha, leaving Maudgalyâyana and another disciple to represent him, went off through the air to the Devaloca, to the Heaven Tus'ita, to preach to the spirits in prison and to convert his mother. When he came down from the mountain (Mienmo), a staircase of glittering diamonds, seen by all, helped his descent. His appearance was blinding. The "six glories" glittered on his person. Mortals and spirits hymned the benign Being who emptied the hells. (Bigandet, p. 209.)

In the Gospel according to the Hebrews is a curious passage, which Baur and Hilgenfeld hold to be the earliest version of the Transfiguration narrative.

"Just now my mother, the Holy Spirit, took me by one of my hairs and bore me up on to the great mountain of Tabor."

This is curious. Buddha and Jesus reach the Mount of Transfiguration, each through the influence of his mother. But perhaps the Jewish writer did not like the universalism inculcated in the Buddhist narrative.

"HE BEGAN TO WASH THE DISCIPLES' FEET."
(John xiii. 5.)

In a vihâra at Gandhâra was a monk so loathsome and stinking, on account of his maladies, that none of his brother disciples dare go near him. The great Teacher came and tended him lovingly and washed his feet. ("Chinese Dhammapada," p. 94.)

THE GREAT BANQUET OF BUDDHA.

In the "Lalita Vistara" (p. 51) it is stated that those who have faith will become "sons of Buddha," and partake of the "food of the kingdom." Four things draw disciples to his banquet,—gifts, soft words, production of benefits, conformity of benefits.

BAPTISM.

In a Chinese life of Buddha by Wung Puh (*see* Beal, "Journ. As. Soc.," vol. xx. p. 172), it is announced that Buddha at Vaisalî delivered a Sûtra, entitled, "The baptism that rescues from life and death and confers salvation."

"AND NONE OF THEM IS LOST BUT THE SON OF PERDITION."

Buddha had also a treacherous disciple, Devadatta. He schemed with a wicked prince, who sent men armed with bows and swords to slaughter Buddha. Devadatta tried other infamous stratagems. His end was appalling. Coming in a palanquin to arrest Buddha, he got out to stretch himself. Suddenly fierce flames burst out and he was carried down to the hell Avichi (the Rayless Place). There, in a red-hot cauldron, impaled by one red bar and pierced by two others, he will stay for a whole Kalpa. Then he will be forgiven. (Bigandet, p. 244.)

THE LAST SUPPER.

Buddha had his last supper or repast with his disciples. A treacherous disciple changed his alms-bowl, and apparently he was poisoned. (*See* Rockhill's "Buddha," p. 133.) Fierce pains seized him as he journeyed afterwards. He was forced to rest. He sent a message to his host, Kunda, the son of the jeweller, to feel no remorse although the feast had been his death. Under two trees he now died.

It will be remembered that during the last supper of Jesus a treacherous disciple "dipped into his dish," but as Jesus was not poisoned, the event had no sequence.

"NOW FROM THE SIXTH HOUR THERE WAS DARKNESS OVER ALL THE LAND UNTIL THE NINTH HOUR."

The critical school base much of their contention that the gospels do not record real history on this particular passage. They urge that such an astounding event could not have escaped Josephus and

Tacitus. When Buddha died, the "sun and moon withdrew their shining," and dust and ashes fell like rain. "The great earth quaked throughout. The crash of the thunder shook the heavens and the earth, rolling along the mountains and valleys." ("Fo-sho-hing-tsan-king," v. 26.) The Buddhist account is certainly not impossible, for the chronicler takes advantage of the phenomena of an Indian dust-storm to produce his dark picture. At Lucknow, before the siege, I remember a storm so dense at midday that some ladies with my regiment thought the Day of Judgment had arrived.

"AND MANY BODIES OF THE SAINTS WHICH SLEPT AROSE."

When Buddha died at Kus'inagara, Ananda and another disciple saw many denizens of the unseen world in the city, by the river Yigdan. (Rockhill's "Life of the Buddha," p. 133.)

"TO ANOINT MY BODY TO THE BURYING." (Mark xiv. 8.)

The newly discovered fragments of the Gospel of Peter give striking evidence of the haphazard way in which extracts from the Buddhist books seem to have been sprinkled among the gospels. It records that Mary Magdalene, "taking with her her friends," went to the sepulchre of Jesus to "place themselves beside him and perform the rites" of wailing, beating breasts, etc. Amrapalî and other courtesans did the same rites to Buddha, and the disciples were afterwards indignant that impure women should have "washed his dead body with their tears." (Rockhill, "Thibetan Life," p. 153.)

In the Christian records are three passages, all due, I think, to the Buddhist narrative. In one, "a woman" anoints Jesus; in John (xii. 7), "Mary" anoints him; in Luke, a "sinner," who kisses and washes his feet with her hair. Plainly these last passages are quite irrational. No woman could have performed the washing and other burial rites on a man alive and in health.

"THEY PARTED MY GARMENTS."

The Abbé Huc tells us ("Voyages," ii. p. 278) that on the death of the Bokté Lama his garments are cut into little strips and prized immensely.

"HE APPEARED UNTO MANY."

Buddha prophesied that he would appear after his death. ("Lotus," p. 144.) In a Chinese version quoted by Eitel ("Three Lectures," p. 57), Buddha to soothe his mother, who had come down weeping from the skies, opens his coffin lid and appears to her In the temple sculptures he is constantly depicted coming down to the altar during worship. (*See* illustrations to my "Buddhism in Christendom.")

THE "GREAT WHITE THRONE."

Mr. Upham, in his "History of Buddhism" (pp. 56,

57), gives a description of the Buddhist heaven. There is a "high mountain," and a city "four square" with gates of gold and silver, adorned with precious stones. Seven moats surround the city. Beyond the last one is a row of marble pillars studded with jewels. The great throne of the god stands in the centre of a great hall, and is surmounted by a white canopy. Round the great throne are seated heavenly ministers, who record men's actions in a "golden book." A mighty tree is conspicuous in the garden. In the Chinese heaven is the "Gem Lake," by which stands the peach tree whose fruit gives immortality.

THE ATONEMENT.

The idea of transferred good Karma, the merits of the former lives of an individual being passed on to another individual, is of course quite foreign to the lower Judaism, which believed in no after life at all. In the view of the higher Buddhism, Sakya Muni saved the world by his teaching, but to the lower, the Buddhism of offerings and temples and monks, this doctrine of Karma was the life-blood. It was proclaimed that Buddha had a vast stock of superfluous Karma, and that offerings at a temple might cause the worshipper in his next life to be a prince instead of a pig or a coolie. In the "Lalita Vistara" (Chinese version, p. 225) it is announced that when Buddha overcame Mâra all flesh rejoiced, the blind saw, the deaf heard, the dumb spake, the hells were cleared, and all by reason of Buddha's Karma in previous lives.

In Romans (v. 18), St. Paul writes thus:—

"As by the offence of one, judgment came upon all men to condemnation, even so by the righteousness of one the free gift came upon all men unto justification of life.

"For as by one man's disobedience many were made sinners, so by the obedience of one shall many be made righteous."

Here plainly all the world is saved by the Karma of Christ.

Now Dr. Kuenen, whose main proposition is that Christianity emerged from Judaism alone, should tell us how Paul got this idea. The priests and the Levites were the sole interpreters of the law, and they had settled that a certain Hebrew had so broken that law that it was necessary to execute him. And now another Hebrew proclaims that the righteousness of this man is so great that he can bestow the "free gift of life" to "all men." Would not Caiaphas have called the second Hebrew out of his mind.

But St. Paul was a Pharisee, and as a Pharisee he knew that the Pharisees that he tried to convert believed that nothing but blood could wipe out sin. In the person of Christ he mixed up the two ideas.

"Whom God hath set forth to be a propitiation through faith in His blood, to declare His righteousness for the remission of sins that are past, through the forbearance of God." (Rom. iii. 25.)

But according to our first quotation, Christ had already saved "all men" by his righteousness alone. Plainly St. Paul, who viewed the Old Testament as "allegory," "carnal ordinances," "beggarly elements," and so on, never meant his trope about Adam's sin to be taken too literally.

PARABLES.

Buddha taught in parables. I will give one or two. The reader is referred to my "Popular Life of Buddha" for some very beautiful ones.

THE PRODIGAL SON.

A certain man had a son who went away into a far country. There he became miserably poor. The father, however, grew rich, and accumulated much gold and treasure, and many storehouses and elephants. But he tenderly loved his lost son, and secretly lamented that he had no one to whom to leave his palaces and suvernas at his death.

After many years the poor man, in search of food and clothing, happened to come to the country where his father had great possessions. And when he was afar off his father saw him, and reflected thus in his mind: "If I at once acknowledge my son and give to him my gold and my treasures, I shall do him a great injury. He is ignorant and undisciplined; he is poor and brutalised. With one of such miserable inclinations 'twere better to educate the mind little by little. I will make him one of my hired servants."

Then the son, famished and in rags, arrived at the door of his father's house; and seeing a great throne upraised, and many followers doing homage to him who sat upon it, was awed by the pomp and the wealth around. Instantly he fled once more to the highway. "This," he thought, "is the house of the poor man. If I stay at the palace of the king perhaps I shall be thrown into prison."

Then the father sent messengers after his son; who was caught and brought back in spite of his cries and lamentations. When he reached his father's house he fell down fainting with fear, not recognising his father, and believing that he was about to suffer some cruel punishment. The father ordered his servants to deal tenderly with the poor man, and sent two labourers of his own rank of life to engage him as a servant on the estate. They gave him a broom and a basket, and engaged him to clean up the dung-heap at a double wage.

From the window of his palace the rich man watched his son at his work: and disguising himself one day as a poor man, and covering his limbs with dust and dirt, he approached his son and said, "Stay here, good man, and I will provide you with food and clothing. You are honest, you are industrious. Look upon me as your father."

After many years the father felt his end approaching, and he summoned his son and the officers of the king, and announced to them the secret that he had so long kept. The poor man was his son, who in early days had wandered away from him; and now that he was conscious of his former debased condition, and was able to appreciate and retain vast wealth, he was determined to hand over to him his entire treasure. The poor man was astonished at this sudden change of fortune, and overjoyed at meeting his father once more.

The parables of Buddha are reported in the Lotus of the Perfect Law to be veiled from the ignorant by means of an enigmatic form of language. The rich man of this parable, with his throne adorned by flowers and garlands of jewels, is announced to be Tathagata (God), who dearly loves all his children, and has prepared for them vast spiritual treasures. But each son of Tathagata has miserable inclinations. He prefers the dung-heap to the pearl mani. To teach such a man, Tathagata is obliged to employ inferior agents, the monk and the ascetic, and to wean him by degrees from the lower objects of desire. When he speaks himself, he is forced to veil much of his thought, as it would not be understood. His sons feel no joy on hearing spiritual things. Little by little must their minds be trained and disciplined for higher truths.

PARABLE OF THE WOMAN AT THE WELL.

Ananda, a favourite disciple of Buddha, was once athirst, having travelled far. At a well he encountered a girl named Matanga, and asked her to give him some water to drink. But she being a woman of low caste, was afraid of contaminating a holy Brahmana, and refused humbly.

"I ask not for caste, but for water!" said Ananda. His condescension won the heart of the girl Matanga.

It happened that she had a mother cunning in love philtres and weird arts, and when this woman heard how much her daughter was in love, she threw her magic spells round the disciple and brought him to her cave. Helpless, he prayed to Buddha, who forthwith appeared and cast out the wicked demons.

But the girl Matanga was still in wretched plight. At last she determined to repair to Buddha himself and appeal to him.

The Great Physician, reading the poor girl's thought questioned her gently :—

"Supposing that you marry my disciple, can you follow him everywhere ?"

"Everywhere !" said the girl.

"Could you wear his clothes, sleep under the same roof ?" said Buddha, alluding to the nakedness and beggary of the "houseless one."

By slow degrees the girl began to take in his meaning, and at last she took refuge in the Three Great Jewels.

A common objection to Buddhism is that it fails to proclaim the fatherhood of God.

"The loving Fatherof all that lives." (Tsing-tu-wan.)

"Our loving Father and Father of all that breathes." ("Imit. Buddha," p. 67.) ("Daily Manual of the Shaman," cited by Mr. Bowden.)

"I am the Heavenly Father (loka pita Swayambhu), the Healer, the Protector of all creatures." (Kern, "Lotus," p. 310.)

I will give a pretty parable that pictures Buddha as a Father.

PARABLE OF THE BLAZING MANSION.

Once there was an old man, broken, decrepit, but

very rich. He possessed much land and many gold pieces. Moreover, he possessed a large rambling mansion which also showed plain proofs of Time's decay. Its rafters were worm-eaten; its pillars were rotten; its galleries were tumbling down; the thatch on its roof was dry and combustible. Inside this mansion were several hundreds of the old man's servants and retainers, so extensive was the collection of rambling old buildings.

Unfortunately, this mansion possessed only one door.

The old man was also the father of many children —five, ten, twenty, let us say. One day there was a smell of burning, and he ran out by the solitary door. To his horror he saw the thatch in a mass of flame, the rotten old pillars were catching fire one by one, the rafters were blazing like tinder. Inside, his children, whom he loved most tenderly, were romping and amusing themselves with their toys.

The distracted father said to himself, "I will run in and save my children. I will seize them in my strong arms. I will bear them harmless through the falling rafters and the blazing beams!" Then the sad thought seized him that his children were romping and ignorant. "If I tell them that the house is on fire they will not understand me. If I try to seize them they will romp about and try to escape. Alas! not a moment is to be lost!"

Suddenly a bright thought flashed across the old man's mind. "My children are ignorant," he mentally said, "but they love toys and glittering playthings. I will promise them some playthings of unheard-of beauty. Then they will listen to me!"

So the old man shouted out with a loud voice, "Children, children, come out of the house and see these beautiful toys. Chariots with white oven, all gold and tinsel. See these exquisite little antelopes! Whoever saw such goats as these! Children, children, come quickly or they will all be gone!"

Forth from the blazing ruin came the children in hot haste. The word "playthings" was almost the only word that they could understand. Then the fond father, in his great joy at seeing his offspring freed from peril, procured for them some of the most beautiful chariots ever seen. Each chariot had a canopy like a pagoda. It had tiny rails and balustrades, and rows of jingling bells. It was formed of the seven precious substances. Chaplets of glittering pearls were hung aloft upon it; standards and wreaths of the most lovely flowers. Milk-white oxen drew these chariots. The children were astonished when they were placed inside.

The meaning of this parable is thus rendered in the "White Lotus of Dharma." The old man is Tathagata, and his children the blind, suffering children of sin and passion. Tathagata fondly loves them, and would save them from their unhappiness. The old rambling mansion, unsightly, rotten, perilous, is the Domain of Karma, the Domain of Appetite. This old mansion is ablaze with the fire of mortal passions, and hates, and lusts. Tathagata in his "immense compassion" would lead all his beloved children away from this great peril, but they do not understand his language. Their only thought is of tinsel toys and childish pastimes. If he speaks to them of the great inner quickening which makes man conquer human pain, they cannot understand him. If he talks to them of wondrous supernatural gifts accorded to mortals, they turn a deaf ear to him. The tinsel chariots provided for the children of Tathagata are the "Vehicles" of the Buddhist teaching.

CHAPTER IV.

After Buddha's Death.

FROM Buddha's death we turn to Buddha's religion and its progress. And I think the narrative form will help us best, but a few preliminary remarks are necessary.

What is Buddhism?

"The religion of Buddha," says Professor Max Müller in his "Chips from a German Workshop," "was made for a madhouse."

"Buddha," says Sir Monier Williams in his "Buddhism," "altogether ignored in human nature any spiritual aspirations."

Having heard the dictum of Oxford, perhaps it is fair to listen to a real Buddhist. In a work called "Happiness," an anonymous writer sketches his religion.

The teaching of Buddha, as set forth by him, is simple and sublime. There are two states of the soul. call them ego and non-ego—the plane of matter and the plane of spirit—what you will. As long as we live for the ego and its greedy joys, we are feverish, restless, miserable. Happiness consists in the destruction of the ego, by the Bodhi, and Gnosis. This is that interior, that high state of the soul, attained by Fenelon and Wesley, by Mirza the Sufi and Swedenborg, by Spinoza and Amiel.

"The kingdom of God is within you," says Christ.

"In whom are hid the treasures of *sophia* and *gnosis*," says St. Paul.

"The enlightened view both worlds," says Mirza the Sufi, "but the bat flieth about in the darkness without seeing."

"Who speaks and acts with the inner quickening," says Buddha, "has joy for his accompanying shadow. Who speaks and acts without the inner quickening, him sorrow pursues as the chariot wheel the horse."

Let us give here a pretty parable, and let Buddha speak for himself:—

"Once upon a time there was a man born blind, and he said, 'I cannot believe in a world of appearances. Colours bright or sombre exist not. There is no sun, no moon, no stars. None have witnessed such things.' His friends chid him; but he still repeated the same words.

"In those days there was a Rishi who had the inner vision; and he detected on the steeps of the lofty Himalayas four simples that had the power to cure the man who was born blind. He culled them, and, mashing them with his teeth, applied them. Instantly the man who was born blind cried out, 'I see colours and appearances. I see beautiful trees and flowers. I see the bright sun. No one ever saw like this before.'

"Then certain holy men came to the man who was born blind, and said to him, 'You are vain and arrogant and nearly as blind as you were before.

You see the outside of things, not the inside. One whose supernatural senses are quickened sees the lapis-lazuli fields of the Buddhas of the Past, and hears heavenly conch shells sounded at a distance of five yoganas. Go off to a desert, a forest, a cavern in the mountains, and conquer this mean thirst of earthly things.' "

The man who was born blind obeyed; and the parable ends with its obvious interpretation. Buddha is the old Rishi, and the four simples are the four great truths. He weans mankind from the lower life and opens the eyes of the blind.

I think that Sir Monier Williams's fancy, that Buddha ignored the spiritual side of humanity is due to the fact that by the word "knowledge" he conceives the Buddhist to mean knowledge of material facts. That Buddha's conceptions are nearer to the ideas of Swedenborg than of Mill is, I think, proved by the Cingalese book, the Samanna Phala Sutta. Buddha details, at considerable length, the practices of the ascetic, and then enlarges upon their exact object. Man has a body composed of the four elements. It is the fruit of the union of his father and mother. It is nourished on rice and gruel, and may be truncated, crushed, destroyed. In this transitory body his intelligence is enchained. The ascetic, finding himself thus confined, directs his mind to the creation of a freer integument. He represents to himself in thought another body created from this material body—a body with a form, members, and organs. This body, in relation to the material body, is like the sword and the scabbard, or a serpent issuing from a basket in which it is confined. The ascetic, then, purified and perfected, commences to practise supernatural faculties. He finds himself able to pass through material obstacles, walls, ramparts, etc.: he is able to throw his phantasmal appearance into many places at once; he is able to walk upon the surface of water without immersing himself; he can fly through the air like a falcon furnished with large wings; he can leave this world and reach even the heaven of Brahma himself.

Another faculty is now conquered by his force of will, as the fashioner of ivory shapes the tusk of the elephant according to his fancy. He acquires the power of hearing the sounds of the unseen world as distinctly as those of the phenomenal world—more distinctly, in point of fact. Also by the power of Manas he is able to read the most secret thoughts of others, and to tell their characters. He is able to say, "There is a mind that is governed by passion. There is a mind that is enfranchised. This man has noble ends in view. This man has no ends in view." As a child sees his earrings reflected in the water, and says, "Those are my earrings," so the purified ascetic recognises the truth. Then comes to him the faculty of "divine vision," and he sees all that men do on earth and after they die, and when they are again reborn. Then he detects the secrets of the universe, and why men are unhappy, and how they may cease to be so.

I will now quote a conversation between Buddha and some Brahmins which, I think, throws much light on his teaching. It is given in another Cingalese book, the "Tevigga Sutta."

When the teacher was dwelling at Manasâkata in the mango grove, some Brahmins, learned in the three Vedas, came to consult him on the question of union with the eternal Brahma. They ask if they are in the right pathway towards that union. Buddha replies at great length. He suggests an ideal case. He supposes that a man has fallen in love with the "most beautiful woman of the land." Day and night he dreams of her, but has never seen her. He does not know whether she is tall or short, of Brahmin or Sudra caste, of dark or fair complexion; he does not even know her name. The Brahmins are asked if the talk of that man about that woman be wise or foolish. They confess that it is "foolish talk." Buddha then applies the same train of reasoning to them. The Brahmins versed in the three Vedas are made to confess that they have never seen Brahma, that they do not know whether he is tall or short, or anything about him, and that all their talk about union with him is also foolish talk. They are mounting a crooked staircase, and do not know whether it leads to a mansion or a precipice. They are standing on the bank of a river and calling to the other bank to come to them.

Now it seems to me that if Buddha were the uncompromising teacher of atheism that Sir Monier Williams pictures him, he has at this point an admirable opportunity of urging his views. The Brahmins, he would of course contend, knew nothing about Brahma, for the simple reason that no such being as Brahma exists.

But this is exactly the line that Buddha does not

take. His argument is that the Brahmins knew nothing of Brahma, because Brahma is purely spiritual, and they are purely materialistic.

Five "Veils," he shows, hide Brahma from mortal ken. These are—

1. The Veil of Lustful Desire.
2. The Veil of Malice.
3. The Veil of Sloth and Idleness.
4. The Veil of Pride and Self-Righteousness.
5. The Veil of Doubt.

Buddha then goes on with his questionings:—

"Is Brahma in possession of wives and wealth?"

"He is not, Gautama!" answers Vasettha the Brahmin.

"Is his mind full of anger, or free from anger?"

"Free from anger, Gautama!"

"Is his mind full of malice, or free from malice?"

"Free from malice, Gautama!"

"Is his mind depraved or pure?"

"It is pure, Gautama!"

"Has he self-mastery, or has he not?"

"He has, Gautama."

The Brahmins are then questioned about themselves.

"Are the Brahmins versed in the three Vedas in possession of wives and wealth, or are they not?"

"They are, Gautama!"

"Have they anger in their hearts, or have they not?"

"They have, Gautama."

"Do they bear malice, or do they not?"

"They do, Gautama."

"Are they pure in heart, or are they not?"

"They are not, Gautama."

"Have they self-mastery, or have they not?"

"They have not, Gautama."

These replies provoke, of course, the very obvious retort that no point of union can be found between such dissimilar entities. Brahma is free from malice, sinless, self-contained, so, of course, it is only the sinless that can hope to be in harmony with him.

Vasettha then puts this question: "It has been told me, Gautama, that Sramana Gautama knows the way to the state of union with Brahma?"

"Brahma I know, Vasettha!" says Buddha in reply, "and the world of Brahma, and the path leading to it!"

The humbled Brahmins learned in the three Vedas then ask Buddha to "show them the way to a state of union with Brahma."

Buddha replies at considerable length, drawing a sharp contrast between the lower Brahminism and the higher Brahminism, the "householder" and the "houseless one." The householder Brahmins are gross, sensual, avaricious, insincere. They practise for lucre black magic, fortune-telling, cozenage. They gain the ear of kings, breed wars, predict victories, sacrifice life, spoil the poor. As a foil to this, he paints the recluse, who has renounced all worldly things, and is pure, self-possessed, happy.

To teach this "higher life," a Buddha "from time to time is born into the world, blessed and worthy, abounding in wisdom, a guide to erring mortals." He sees the universe face to face, the spirit world of

Brahma and that of Mâra the tempter. He makes his knowledge known to others. The houseless one, instructed by him, "lets his mind pervade one quarter of the world with thoughts of pity sympathy, and equanimity; and so the second, and so the third, and so the fourth. And thus the whole wide world, above, below, around, and everywhere, does he continue to pervade with heart of pity, sympathy, and equanimity, far-reaching, grown great, and beyond measure."

"Verily this, Vasettha, is the way to a state of union with Brahma," and he proceeds to announce that the bhikshu, or Buddhist beggar, "who is free from anger, free from malice, pure in mind, master of himself, will, after death, when the body is dissolved, become united with Brahma." The Brahmins at once see the full force of this teaching. It is as a conservative in their eyes that Buddha figures, and not an innovator. He takes the side of the ancient spiritual religion of the country against rapacious innovators.

Sir Monier Williams quotes a part of this Sutta, and, oddly enough, still maintains that Buddha was an atheist.

There are two great schools of Buddhism, and they are quite agreed on this point that Buddhism is the quickening of the spiritual vision.

Let us now consider how the two great schools of Buddhism diverge.

1. The earliest school, the Buddhism of Buddha, taught that after Nirvâna, or man's emancipation from re-birth, the consciousness of the individual survived, and that he dwelt for ever in happiness in

the Brahma heavens. This is the Buddhism of the "Little Vehicle."

2. The second, or innovating school, maintained that after Nirvâna the consciousness of the individual ceased. Their creed was the blank atheism of the Brahmin S'unyavâdi.

The first serious study of Buddhism took place in one of our colonies, and the first students were missionaries. Great praise is due to the missionaries of Ceylon for their early scholarship, but naturally they ransacked the Buddhist books less as scholars than missionaries. Soon they discovered with delight the teaching of the atheistic school, and statements that the Ceylon scriptures were the earliest authentic Buddhist scriptures, brought to the island by Mahinda, King Asoka's son (B.C. 306). In consequence of this the missionaries concluded that Ceylon had preserved untainted the original teaching of Buddha, and that the earliest school, that of the "Little Vehicle," was atheistic.

But the leading Sanscrit scholar of the world, Dr. Rajendra Lala Mitra, has completly dissipated this idea. In his work, "Nepalese Buddhist Literature," p. 178, he shows conclusively that it is the Buddhism of the innovating school, that of the "Great Vehicle," which preaches atheism. About the epoch of Christ, Kanerkos or Kanishka, a king who conquered India, introduced this innovating teaching. Hweng Thsang, the Chinese pilgrim, who visited India in the seventh century, confirms this. There was in India at this date amongst the followers of Siva, a school who held that Nothingness was God, and Nothingness the future of man. They were called the S'unyavâdis, the proclaimers of Nothingness. Two priests, Parsvika and Vasabandhu, were with Kanerkos, and they persuaded this monarch to force this Pyrrhonism on the Buddhists. A mighty conflict was the consequence. The old Buddhists remonstrated. They said that Buddha knew nothing of all this. They called the "Great Vehicle" Sunyapushpa (the Carriage that drives to Nowhere). But Parsvika packed a convocation like Constantine, and forced the new teaching down their throats. ("Hweng Thsang, Hist." p. 114., *et. seq.* "Memoirs," pp. 174, 220.) Rajendra Lala Mitra says that the Buddhist books of the "Great Vehicle" are in a servile manner copied from Brahmin treatises.

Let us examine this "Great Vehicle," as writers like Sir Monier Williams tells us that it was this school that introduced the ideas of God and immortality into Buddhism, which until then was pure atheism. Its main Bible is a collection of writings called the "Rakshâ Bhagavatî." (Rajendra Lala Mitra, p. 179.) Bryan Hodgson confirms this. ("Literature of Nepal," p. 16.) The work itself is an avowed attack on the Hinayâna or "Little Vehicle," which is "refuted repeatedly," says the learned Hindoo. (P. 178.)

Let us now see what sort of god and what sort of immortality the "Rakshâ Bhagavatî" in its title of chapters proclaimed.

Chap. I. The subject of Nothingness (Sunyata) expounded.

Chap. II. Relation of the soul to form colour and vacuity.

Chap. IV. Relation of form to vacuity

Chap. VII. How a Bodhisattwa merges all natural attributes into vacuity.

Chap. XII. The doctrine of Mahâyâna and its advantages, derived principally, if not entirely, from its recognition of the greatness of S'unyavâda (Nihilistic doctrine of the Brahmin sect of S'unyavâdis).

Chap. XIII. To the Bodhisattwa there is nothing eternal, nothing transient, nothing painful, nothing pleasant. All qualities are unreal as a dream.

Chap. XIV.-XVI. The principle of the Prajnâ Paramitâ imparted by Buddha to Indra. The end sought is the attainment of vacuity.

Chap. XXXV. All objects attainable by the study of Nihilism. ("Nepalese Buddhist Literature," p. 180.)

Hodgson gives a bit of what he calls this "pure Pyrrhonism" from the same book. Buddha is made to talk thus:—

"The being of all things is derived from belief, reliance, in this order: from false knowledge, delusive impression; from delusive impression, general notions; from them, particulars; from them, the six seats of the senses; from them, contact; from it, definite sensation and perception; from it, thirst or desire; from it, embryolic (physical) existence; from it, birth or actual existence; from it, all the distinctions of genus and species among animate things; from them, decay and death, after the manner and period peculiar to each. Such is the procession of all things into existence from delusion (avidyâ), and in the inverse order to that of their procession they retrograde into non-existence." (P. 79.)

Another book, the "Suvarna Prabhâsa," makes "grand non-existence," the Bodhi, the divine knowledge. "I now instruct you on the means of acquiring the knowledge of nothingness," Buddha is made to say to his disciples. (Rajendra Lala Mitra, p. 243.)

But there is a third school of Buddhism, the Madhyamika, or "Middle Pathway." Unless all this is definitely understood, Buddhism will remain a riddle. For a long time the "Great" and the "Little" Vehicles fought furiously. I believe that the "Middle Pathway" was a rude attempt at conciliation. No one can read many Buddhist writings without observing flat contradictions at every page. Thus the Brahmajâla Sûtra, much quoted by missionaries, who are plainly unaware that it belongs to the literature of the "Carriage that drives to Nowhere," announces that the existence of the soul after death in a conscious or even an unconscious state is impossible. But there is a passage which the missionaries do not quote. Buddha also tells his disciples that the statement of the Brahmins and Buddhist teachers, that "existing beings are cut off, destroyed, annihilated," is founded on their ignorance and want of perception of the truth. (*See* my "Popular Life of Buddha," p. 223.)

Having thus cleared the way, I will now proceed with the history of the progress of Buddha's religion. Before, it would have been unintelligible.

Buddha died B.C. 470. Asoka, the Buddhist Constantine, gained India B.C. 260. Unfortunately, between these two dates there is scarcely any authentic history at all. Buddha left behind him brief instructions to his disciples, which are called the "Twelve Observances." They were never to sleep under a roof. In Ceylon even to this day a Buddhist monk is called Abhyâvakâsika (he whose covering is the heavens). They were never to stop two nights in the same spot. What was to be their food? Refuse victuals. What was to be their dress? Rags from the graveyard, dung-heap, etc. What was his following to be called? The "Mob of Beggars" (Bhikshu Sangha). Jumping from B.C. 470 to B.C. 302, history flashes a sudden light upon these wandering beggars.

At this date Seleucus Nicator sent an ambassador named Megasthenes to King Chandragupta at Patna. His account of the India of that day is, unfortunately, lost; but through Diodorus Siculus, Strabo, Arrian, and Clement of Alexandria, some valuable fragments have come down to us. Patna, it must be remembered, was in the heart of the Buddhist Holy Land. Clement of Alexandria cites a passage from Megasthenes about the Indian "philosophers." "Of these there are two classes, some of them called Sarmanæ (Sramanas) and other Brahmins. And those of the Sarmanæ, who are called Hylobii, neither inhabit cities nor have roofs over them, but are clothed in the bark of trees, feed on nuts, and drink water in their hands. Like those called Encratites in the present day, they know not marriage, nor begetting of children. Some, too, of the Indians obey the precepts of Buddha, whom, on account of his extraordinary sanctity, they have raised to divine honours."

Strabo also describes the Brahmins and the Hylobii, or Germanes, with similar details. He draws a distinction between the Germanes and the Brahmins on the subject of continency, the Brahmins being polygamists.

No doubt these Sarmanæ and Brahmins of Megasthenes were the Brahmins and Buddhist Sramanas, or ascetics. To the first were confided sacrifices and ceremonies. They were a caste apart, and none outside this caste could officiate. Their ideas of life and death, it is announced, were similar to those of Plato and the Greeks. The Brahmins ate flesh and had many wives. Every new year there was a great synod of them. They dwelt in groves near the great cities on "couches of leaves and skins."

The Hylobii, on the other hand, insisted on absolute continence and strict vegetarianism, and water drinking. Clitarchus gives us an additional fact from Megasthenes. The Hylobii "derided the Brahmins." "By their means," says Strabo, "kings serve and worship God." (See for all that can be recovered from Megasthenes, Cory, "Ancient Fragments," pp. 225-227.)

That the Buddhists at first were wandering beggars without any convents is the opinion of the Russian Orientalist, Wassiljew, who supports it from a valuable Chinese history by Daranatha. It asserts that the King Ajatasatru passed Varsha or Lent in a graveyard; and that until the date of Upagupta, a contemporary of Asoka, there were no temples. The first was built at Mathura. (Ch. iv., cited by Wassiljew, "Buddhism," p. 41.)

Daranatha asserts that a disciple of Ananda reached Cashmir. M. Wassiljew remarks that this would mean a spread of the doctrines in intermediate lands. I must point out that the first ritual of Buddhism was the "Praise of the Seven Mortal Buddhas," who were worshipped, as Gen. Cunningham has shown from the Bharhut Stupa, in the form of trees. This seems to have been the sole form of worship even in the days of King Asoka, who enjoins his subjects to worship round Buddha's tree, the ficus indicus.

I think that my readers are now in a position to judge whether India was gained by houseless Parivrajakas, ever marching, ever preaching, ever enduring hunger, thirst, buffets, death if necessary, or by lazy monks, living in sumptuous convents, and debating whether their couches should have fringes and their dress be silk or cotton. This last is the contention of the Buddhist histories, and these dishonest documents have even deceived learned men in the West, more skilful in Pâli roots, perhaps, than judicial analysis. These books record that three months after Buddha's death a vast convocation of monks was assembled at Râjâgriha to render canonical certain holy books, in bulk four times as big as our Bible. Eighteen disused monasteries were hastily cleared of their cobwebs and rubbish, and set in order for these monks, and a cave temple, whose columns and splendid stone carvings vied with Ellora, was cut out of the rock in what must be thought a very small space of time, namely, two months. I have shown in my "Popular Life of Buddha" that we have here most probably the details of a real convocation, that of King Kanerkos, assembled about 20 A.D., by the "Carriage that drives Nowhere" (Sunyapushpa) to force their Pyrrhonism on the old faith, and that they have dishonestly antedated this convocation by nearly 500 years, to make it appear that their innovations were the earliest Buddhism. Hweng Thsang, the Chinese pilgrim, has given us the details of the convocation.

The number of monks was fixed at four hundred and ninety-nine. The ambitious Vasubandhu, leader of the "Great Vehicle" movement, presented himself at the door, but the traditions of early Buddhism were still strong. Some of the monks desired him to depart, as none but Arhats (the fully enfranchised) could remain near the building.

"I care little for the enfranchisement of study" (the rank of Arhat), said Vasubandhu. Then, with some inconsistency, he performed a great miracle to prove that he had attained that dignity. He flung into the air a ball of thread, and one end remained fixed in the sky. A similar prodigy was witnessed by Marco Polo and other old travellers. Vasubandhu was chosen president, and the convocation proceeded to discuss their Pyrrhonism. All this is servilely repeated in the fictitious narrative of the first convocation. A difficulty arose about Ananda, who had not acquired the miraculous powers that stamp the adept in the knowledge of Prajñâ Pâramitâ, the wisdom of the unseen world. Thus, as first constituted, the convocation consisted of 499 members and a vacant carpet was spread for Ananda. During the night he meditated on the Kâyagastâ Sâtiyâ, and in the morning these powers came; and in proof he reached his seat through the medium of the floor of the temple.

To culminate this silliness, Ananda is then called

upon to disclose this "wisdom of the unseen world," because, being Buddha's chief disciple, he is the only one who knows much about it. The Bible of the "Carriage that drives Nowhere" is the chief book discussed, the Brahmajâla Sûtra, which Hoa Yen, the greatest Chinese authority (*see* Rémusat, "Pilgrimage of Fa Hian," p. 108), says is distinctly a "Great Vehicle" scripture. In it Buddha discusses every conceivable theory about the next world, and contradicts them all. Could such an insane Bible, in a few years, have tumbled to pieces the great priesthoods of India, China, Persia?

We now come to King Asoka, a monarch whose dominions stretched from Grândhâra, or Peshawur, to Chola and Pândiya, the extreme southern provinces of India. On the extreme west he cut a rock-inscription at Girnar, on the Gulf of Cutch. On the east coast at Ganjam were the Dhauli and Jaugada inscriptions. His rule was a broad one.

He became a convert to Buddhism, and made it the official creed. He carved his "Edicts" on rocks and stone columns. Let us see from them whether early Buddhism was the atheism and negation of an immortal life that is depicted in popular treatises. He is called Devânampiya, the friend of the spirits.

KING ASOKA'S IDEAS ABOUT GOD.

"Much longing after the things [of this life] is a disobedience, I again declare; not less so is the laborious ambition of dominion by a prince who would be a propitiator of Heaven. Confess and believe in God [Isâna], who is the worthy object of obedience. For equal to this [belief], I declare unto you, ye shall not find such a means of propitiating Heaven. Oh, strive ye to obtain this inestimable treasure." (First separate Edict, Dhauli, Prinsep.)

"Thus spake King Devânampiya Piyadasi:—The present moment and the past have departed under the same ardent hopes. How by the conversion of the royal born may religion be increased? Through the conversion of the lowly born if religion thus increaseth, by how much [more] through the conviction of the high born and their conversion shall religion increase? Among whomsoever the name of God resteth, verily this is religion."

"Thus spake Devânampiya Piyadasi:—Wherefore from this very hour I have caused religious discourses to be preached. I have appointed religious observances that mankind, having listened thereto, shall be brought to follow in the right path, and give glory to God." (Edict No. vii., Prinsep.)

ASOKA ON A FUTURE LIFE.

"On the many beings over whom I rule I confer happiness in this world; in the next they may obtain Swarga [paradise]." (Edict vi., Wilson.)

"This is good. With these means let a man seek Swarga. This is to be done. By these means it is to be done, as by them Swarga [paradise] is to be gained." (Edict ix., Wilson.)

"I pray with every variety of prayer for those who differ with me in creed, that they, following after my example, may with me attain unto eternal salvation." (Delhi Pillar, Edict vi., Prinsep.)

"And whoso doeth this is blessed of the inhabitants of this world; and in the next world endless moral merit resulteth from such religious charity." (Edict xi., Prinsep.)

"Unto no one can be repentance and peace of mind until he hath obtained supreme knowledge, perfect faith, which surmounteth all obstacles, and perpetual assent." (Rock Edict, No. vii., Prinsep.)

"In the tenth year of his anointment, the beloved King Piyadasi obtained the Sambodhi or complete knowledge." (Rock Edict, No. vii., Burnouf.)

"All the heroism that Piyadasi, the beloved of the gods, has exhibited is in view of another life. Earthly glory brings little profit, but, on the contrary, produces a loss of virtue. To toil for heaven is difficult to peasant and to prince unless by a supreme effort he gives up all." (Rock Edict, No. x., Burnouf.)

"May they [my loving subjects] obtain happiness in this world and in the next." (Second separate Edict, Burnouf.)

Early Buddhism had no prayer, no worship, say our popular treatises.

"Devânampiya has also said—Fame consisteth in this act, to meditate with devotion on my motives and on my deeds, and to pray for blessings in this world and the world to come." (Dhauli, separate Edict, No. ii., Prinsep.)

"I pray with every variety of prayer for those who differ with me in creed, that they, following after my example, may with me attain unto eternal salvation." (Delhi Pillar, Edict vi., Prinsep.)

Early Buddhism knew nothing of soul, we learn also. "As the soul itself, so is the unrelaxing guidance of Devânampiya worthy of respect." (Dhauli, separate Edict, No. ii., Prinsep.)

On the Bairât rock the king, too, gives a list of the holy books that his monks were to learn by heart.

1. The Summary of Discipline.
2. The Supernatural Powers of the Masters.
3. The Terrors of the Future.
4. The Song of the Muni.
5. The Sûtra on Asceticism.
6. The Question of Upatishya.
7. The Admonition to Râhula concerning Falsehood, uttered by our Lord Buddha.

Nothing can be more important than this. If the Bairât rock-inscription is genuine, the Ceylon history of the convocations is pure fiction.

It must be remembered that in the old Indian creeds, holy books were handed down entirely by recitation. The letters of the alphabet, according to Professor Max Müller, General Cunningham, and the chief authorities, were not known in India until Asoka's day. We know from the Mahâwanso that the holy books of Ceylon were not committed to writing until the reign of King Wattaganini (104 to 76 B.C.). So the books that Asoka ordered to be handed down by the recitation and chantings of his monks must have plainly constituted the entire body of the recognised scriptures. In what way could any other scriptures come down? Dr. Oldenburg talks of these seven books as if they were "passages" only, he believing that the large body of Pâli scriptures of Ceylon were in existence as early as the second convocation. But if they were "passages," who was to remember and recite the rest of the voluminous canon? Asoka's monks were expressly forbidden so to do.

Of immense importance is one more fact. The Dhauli inscription announces that the four Greek kings (Chapta Yoni Raja), who took over Alexander's empire, had allowed their subjects to "follow the doctrine" of Asoka. He mentions Antiochus and Ptolemy. Also "Gongakenos" and Megas of Cyrene. This plainly proves that his missionaries had reached Egypt and Greece.

CHAPTER V.

The Apostles of the Bloodless Altar.

THERE are two Zoroasters, or rather a sort of dual personality. One of these Zoroasters lived six thousand years B.C. according to Darmesteter, and the other about five hundred years B.C. The earlier Zoroaster swathed Persia in a network of silly rites and regulations. A culprit who "threw away a dead dog" was to receive a thousand blows with the horse goad, and one thousand with the Craosha charana. A culprit who slew a dog with a "prickly back" and a "woolly muzzle" was to receive a similar punishment." ("Fargard," xxx.) This Zoroaster was particular about the number of gnats, ants, lizards, that the devout had to kill. ("Fargard," xiv.) This Zoroaster proclaimed a god who loved to see on his altar a "hundred horses, a thousand cows, ten thousand small cattle," and so on. ("Khordah Avesta," xii.) But the second Zoroaster proclaimed a bloodless altar, and sought to tear the network of the first Zoroaster to shreds. What was the meaning of this? Simply that the Buddhist Wanderers had by this time invaded Persia, and had fastened their doctrines upon the chief local prophet. This was their habit. A study of this second religion, the religion of Mithras, will help us to some of the secrets of Buddhist propagandism.

Mr. Felix Oswald cites Wassiljew as announcing that the Buddhist missionaries had reached Western Persia, B.C. 450. This date would, of course, depend on the date of Buddha's life and Buddha's death. The latter is now definitely fixed by Buhler's translation of Asoka's Rupnath rock-inscription, B.C. 470. Wassiljew, citing Daranatha, announces that Madeantica, a convert of Ananda, Buddha's leading disciple, reached Ouchira in Cashmir. From Cashmir Buddhism passed promptly to Candahar and Cabul. (P. 40). Thence it penetrated quickly to Bactra, and soon invaded "all the country embraced by the word Turkistan, where it flourished until disturbed by Mahomet."

Tertullian has two passages which describe the religion of Mithras.

He says that the devil, to "pervert the truth," by "the mystic rites of his idols vies even with the essential portions of the sacraments of God. He too baptises some—that is, his own believers and faithful followers. He promises the putting away of sins by a laver (of his own), and, if my memory still serves me, Mithras there (in the kingdom of Satan) sets his mark on the foreheads of his soldiers, celebrates also the oblation of bread, and introduces an image of the resurrection, and before a sword wreathes a crown." (Pres. v., Hœr. chap. xl.)

Here is another passage.

"Some soldier of Mithras, who at his initiation in the gloomy cavern,—in the camp, it may well be said, of darkness,—when at the sword's point a sword is presented to him as though in mimicry of martyrdom, and thereupon a crown is put upon his head, is admonished to resist and cast it off, and, if you like, transfer it to his shoulders, saying that Mithras is his crown. He even has his virgins and his ascetics (continentes). Let us take note of the devices of the devil, who is wont to ape some of God's things." ("De Corona," xv.)

From this it is plain that the worshippers of Mithras had the simple rites of Buddhists and Christians, baptism and the bloodless altar; also an early Freemasonry, which some detect veiled in the Indian life of Buddha. Thus the incident of the sword and crown in the Mithraic initiation is plainly based on the menacing sword of Mâra in the "Lalita Vistara" and the crown that he offered Buddha. In modern masonry it is feigned that Hiram Abiff, the architect of Solomon's temple, made three efforts to escape from three assassins. These are plainly Old Age, Disease, and Death. He sought to evade the first at the east of the temple, in the same way that Buddha tried to escape by the eastern gate. The second and third flights of Hiram and Buddha were to the same points of the compass. Then Buddha escaped the lower life through the Gate of Benediction, and Hiram was killed. The disciples of Mithras had, in the comedy of their initiation, "seven tortures,"—heat, cold, hunger, thirst, fire, water, etc.,—experiences by no means confined to histrionics in the experience of Buddha's Wanderers. A modern mason goes through the comedy of giving up his gold and silver and baring his breast and feet, a form that once had a meaning. Mithras was born in a cave; and at Easter there was the ceremony called by Tertullian the "image of the resurrection." The worshippers, Fermicus tells us ("De Errore," xxiii.), placed by night a stone image on a bier in a cave and went through the forms of mourning. The dead god was then placed in a tomb, and after a time withdrawn from it. Then lights were lit, and poems of rejoicing sounded out, and the priest comforted the devotees. "You shall have salvation from your sorrows!" Dupuis naturally compares all this to the *cierge pascal* and Catholic rites. In Jerusalem the Greek pontiff goes into the cave called Christ's sepulchre and brings out miraculous fire to the worshippers, who are fighting and biting each other outside, imaging unconsciously Buddha's great battle with Mâra and the legions of hell, its thunder and lightning and turmoil, followed by a bright coruscation, and by the angels who greeted his victory. This sudden illumination, which is the chief rite of Freemasonry, of Mithraism, and of Christianity, has oddly enough been thrown overboard by the English Church.

That Mithraism was at once Freemasonry and Buddhism is proved by its great spread. Buddhism was the first missionary religion. Judaism and the other old priestcrafts were for a "chosen people." At the epoch of Christ, Mithraism had already honeycombed the Roman paganism. Experts have discovered its records in Arthur's Oon and other British caves.

A similar Freemasonry was Pythagoreanism in Greece. Colebrooke, the prince of Orientalists, saw at once that its philosophy was purely Buddhist. Its rites were identical with those of the Mithraists and Essenes. These last must now be considered. They have this importance, that they are due to a separate propagandism. Alexandria was built by the great invader of India, to bridge the east and the west. And an exceptional toleration of creeds was the result.

Neander divides Israel at the date of Christ into three sections:—

1. Pharisaism, the "dead theology of the letter."

2. Sadduceeism, "debasing of the spiritual life into worldliness."

3. Essenism, Israel mystical—a "co-mingling of Judaism with the old Oriental theosophy."

Concerning this latter section, Philo wrote a letter to a man named Hephæstion, of which the following is a portion:—

"I am sorry to find you saying that you are not likely to visit Alexandria again. This restless, wicked city can present but few attractions, I grant, to a lover of philosophic quiet. But I cannot commend the extreme to which I see so many hastening. A passion for ascetic seclusion is becoming daily more prevalent among the devout and the thoughtful, whether Jew or Gentile. Yet surely the attempt to combine contemplation and action should not be so soon abandoned. A man ought at least to have evinced some competency for the discharge of the social duties before he abandons them for the divine. First the less, then the greater.

"I have tried the life of the recluse. Solitude brings no escape from spiritual danger. If it closes some avenues of temptation, there are few in whose case it does not open more. Yet the Therapeutæ, a sect similar to the Essenes, with whom you are acquainted, number many among them whose lives are truly exemplary. Their cells are scattered about the region bordering on the farther shore of the Lake Mareotis. The members of either sex live a single and ascetic life, spending their time in fasting and contemplation, in prayer or reading. They believe themselves favoured with divine illumination—an inner light. They assemble on the Sabbath for worship, and listen to mystical discourses on the traditionary lore which they say has been handed down in secret among themselves. They also celebrate solemn dances and processions of a mystic significance by moonlight on the shore of the great mere. Sometimes, on an occasion of public rejoicing, the margin of the lake on our side will be lit with a fiery chain of illuminations, and galleys, hung with lights, row to and fro with strains of music sounding over the broad water. Then the Therapeutæ are all hidden in their little hermitages, and these sights and sounds of the world they have abandoned make them withdraw into themselves and pray.

"Their principle at least is true. The soul which is occupied with things above, and is initiated into the mysteries of the Lord, cannot but account the body evil, and even hostile. The soul of man is divine, and his highest wisdom is to become as much as possible a stranger to the body with its embarrassing appetites.

God has breathed into man from heaven a portion of His own divinity. That which is divine is invisible. It may be extended, but it is incapable of separation. Consider how vast is the range of our thought over the past and the future, the heavens and the earth. This alliance with an upper world, of which we are conscious, would be impossible, were not the soul of man an indivisible portion of that divine and blessed spirit. Contemplation of the divine essence is the noblest exercise of man; it is the only means of attaining to the highest truth and virtue, and therein to behold God is the consummation of our happiness here."

Here we have the higher Buddhism, which seeks to reach the plane of spirit, an "alliance with the upper world" by the aid of solitary reverie. That Philo knew where this religion had come from is, I think, proved by another passage.

"Among the Persians there is the order of Magi who deeply investigate the works of nature for the discovery of truth, and in leisure's quiet are initiated into and expound in clearest significance the divine virtues.

"In India, too, there is the sect of the Gymnosophists, who, in addition to speculative philosophy, diligently cultivate the ethical also, and have made their life an absolute ensample of virtue.

"Palestine, moreover, and Syria are not without their harvest of virtuous excellence, which region is inhabited by no small portion of the very populous nation of the Jews. There are counted amongst them certain ones, by name Essenes, in number about four thousand, who derive their name, in my opinion, by an inaccurate trace from the term in the Greek language for holiness (Essen or Essaios—Hosios, holy), inasmuch as they have shown themselves pre-eminent by devotion to the service of God; not in the sacrifice of living animals, but rather in the determination to make their own minds fit for a holy offering." (Philo, "Every virtuous man is free.")

Plainly here the Essenes are pronounced of the same faith as the Gymnosophists of India, who abstain from the bloody sacrifice, that is the Buddhists.

I will now jot hastily down the points of contact between one of these monasteries described by Philo and a Buddhist monastery. In the centre is the sanctuary. Round it, in an enclosure "four square," are ranged the cells of the monks. The monks in Thibet, according to the Abbé Huc, may be divided into three categories.

1. Those who live in monasteries and perform the religious services, and also, like the Essenes described by Josephus, farm the convent land.

2. Hermits, in caves, like Banos dreaming holy dreams.

3. Wandering missionaries (Parivrajakas) who, like the "Apostles" described in the recently discovered "Teaching of the Twelve Apostles," are not allowed to remain more than a day in the same place.

In the Buddhist Lent the community goes into a hastily built group of mud huts in the jungle. Each of these is tenanted by a monk and two novices. Each has a "guest chamber" for a sick man, or a wandering beggar. This throws light on much. Let us continue our parallelism.

Enforced vegetarianism, community of goods, rigid abstinence from sexual indulgence, also a high standard of purity, were common to both the Buddhists and the Therapeuts.

Neither community allowed the use of wine.

Long fastings were common to both.

With both, silence was a special spiritual discipline.

The Therapeut left "for ever," says Philo, "brothers, children, wives, father and mother," for the contemplative life.

Like the Buddhists, the Therapeuts had nuns vowed to chastity.

The preacher and the missionary, two original ideas of Buddhism, were conspicuous amongst the Therapeuts. This was in direct antagonism to the spirit of Mosaism.

The Therapeut was a healer of the body as well as the soul.

Turning to the kindred society of the Essenes we get a few additional points of contact.

The Essenes, like the Buddhist monks, had ridiculous laws relating to spitting and other natural acts, those of the Essenes being regulated by a superstitious veneration for the Sabbath day, those of the Buddhists, by a superstitious respect for a pagoda.

In Buddhist monasteries a rigid obedience, together with a quite superstitious respect for the person of a superior, is enacted. In Buddhaghosa's Parables is a puerile story of a malicious Muni, who, when an inferior monk had gone out of a hut where the two were sleeping, lay across the doorway in order to make the novice inadvertently commit the great sin of placing his foot above his superior's head. The penalty of such an act is that the offender's head ought to be split into seven pieces. With the Essenes similar superstitions were rife. If an Approacher accidentally touched the hem of the garment of an Associate, all sorts of purifications had to be gone through.

The principle of thrift and unsavouriness in dress was carried to extremes by both Essenes and Buddhists. The sramana (ascetic) was required to stitch together for his *kowat* the refuse rags acquired by begging. The Essenes were expected to wear the old clothes of their co-religionists until they tumbled to pieces.

In the Thibetan "Life of Buddha," by Rockhill, it is announced that when the great teacher first cast off his kingly silks he donned a foul dress that had been previously worn by ten other saints. This throws light on the story of Elisha.

Dr. Ginsburg ("The Essenes," p. 13) shows that the Essenes had eight stages of progress in inner or spiritual knowledge.

1. Outward or bodily purity by baptism.

2. The state of purity that has conquered the sexual desire.

3. Inward and spiritual purity.

4. A meek and gentle spirit which has subdued all anger and malice.

5. The culminating point of holiness.

6. The body becomes the temple of the Holy Ghost, and the mystic acquires the gift of prophecy.

7. Miraculous powers of healing, and of raising the dead.

8. The mystic state of Elias.

The Buddhists have likewise eight stages of inner progress, the Eightfold Holy Path. The first step, "Those who have entered the stream, the Nairañjana, the mystic river of Buddha, is precisely the same as the first Essene step. Then follow advances in purity, holiness, and mastery of passion. In the last two stages the Buddhists, like the Essenes, gained supernatural powers, to be used in miraculous cures, prophecies, and other occult marvels. It must be mentioned that the Essenes were circumcised as well as the other Jews.

The word "Essenes," according to some learned philologists, means the "Bathers," or "Baptisers," baptism having been their initiatory rite. Josephus tells us that this baptism was not administered until the aspirant had remained a whole year outside the community, but "subjected to their rule of life."

I will here give the rite of Buddhist baptism (abhisheka) when a novice is about to become a monk. It consists of many washings, borrowed plainly by the early Buddhists from the Brahmins, and brings to mind the frequent use of water attributed to the Hemero Baptists or disciples of John. It may be mentioned that in some Buddhist countries —Nepal, for instance—the various monkish vows are now taken only for form sake. This makes the letter, retained after the spirit has departed, all the more valuable.

The neophyte having made an offer of scents and

unguents (betel-nut, paun, etc.) to his spiritual guide (guru), the latter, after certain formalities, draws four circles in the form of a cross, in honour of the Tri Ratna (trinity), on the ground, and the neophyte, seated in a prescribed position, recites the following text: "I salute Lord Buddha, Dharma, and Sangha, and entreat them to bestow on me the Pravrajya Vrata." The first and second days of the ceremonial are consumed in prayers and formalities carried on by the guide and his pupil alone. On the second day another mystical cross is drawn on the ground, the Swastica. A pot containing water and other mystic ingredients, a gold lotus, and certain confections and charms, figure in these early rites. At last it is poured on the neophyte's head. This is the baptism.

Previous to this there is a confession of sins and much catechising. The catechumen's name is changed at the baptism, and his head is shaved. A light is lit which reminds one of the φωτισμός of the early Christians. Besides their baptism, the Essenes and Therapeuts had a mystery (sacramentum), an oblation of bread. Part of this was placed upon the bloodless altar, and part eaten. The Buddhists with their wheat and rice do exactly the same thing.

Two other points remain, the most important of all. The Buddhists have a Trinity, Buddha or Swayambhu, the Self-Existent, Dharma or Prajnâ, which is the same word as Philo's Sophia Wisdom. From these two the Father and the Mother have been produced. Sangha, literally Union, the union of matter and spirit, like St. Paul's Christ, Humanity—ideal Humanity.

That a nation so "stiff-necked" as the Jews in the

matter of their one God, should have accepted a Trinity, shows certainly a foreign influence.

The second point is stronger still. The Buddhist teachers in Persia and Egypt in days before Christ; in Japan, in Islâm, during the Middle Ages; in Europe now,—have had and have one method of procedure. They say practically, "Religion as we conceive it has only one lesson—knowledge of God. This is to be acquired not externally through creeds and priests, but internally by the education and purification of the soul. Keep your Bibles if the weaker brethren insist on them, but explain that they are symbols, not history. Keep your prophets, your Moses, your Mahomet, your Zoroaster, and fasten our teaching on him. Keep your hob-goblins and folklore, but give up your bloody altar."

Now, in the view of the Jew, God had made a covenant with Israel, which was to last as long as the sun, the moon, and the stars. In return for the "offerings of the Lord made by fire" (Levit. xxiv. 9) on the temple altar of Jerusalem, Israel was to triumph over its foes and receive every temporal blessing. The advice of the Buddhist was practically that the Jewish half of the bargain was to be broken, but that the Bible, the document containing the contract, was to be retained. *A priori* could any one have guessed that advice of this sort could be taken?

And yet we see the Essenes "allegorize" the bloody altar out of their Bible, but cling to the document more fondly than ever. The early Christians and Justin and Irenæus do the same. Scripture for the early Church was the Old Testament.

CHAPTER VI.

The Gospel according to the Hebrews.

PAPIAS, the Bishop of Hieropolis (about A.D. 140), wrote a small sentence which, examined critically recently, has revolutionised all our ideas about the four eye-witnesses of Paley.

He tells us that Matthew first in the Hebrew dialect wrote the λόγια (sayings), and each person translated as he was able.

This tells us everything. Matthew in Aramaic wrote down all the "sayings" of Christ that he could remember, and our three gospels and a number of other gospels were translations, enlargements, and fanciful versions of this. Matthew's work emerged in the Church at Jerusalem, and was their sole scripture. Jerome (416 A.D.), writing against the Pelagians, says:

"In the Gospel according to the Hebrews—which is written, indeed, in the Chaldee and Syriac language, but in Hebrew letters, which the Nazarenes use to this day—according to the Apostles, or, as very many deem, according to Matthew." ("Dial. adv. Pelag.," ch. iii.)

This gives us its title. The Gospel according to the Hebrews was first called the Gospel according to the Apostles, and sometimes the Gospel according to Matthew. What do we know about this Gospel according to the Apostles? In a great trial, three or four obscure witnesses often unexpectedly assume a dominant importance. In the great trial now going on of Christianity (as distinguished from the religion of Christ), four such witnesses have suddenly surged up.

They are Hegesippus, Papias, Justin Martyr, Irenæus. What do they tell us of the Gospel of the Apostles—the Gospel according to the Hebrews?

Hegesippus (170 A.D.) was the earliest Church historian, but his history has been destroyed. Eusebius tells us ("Hist.," iv. 22) that he was a Jew, and that he used the Gospel according to the Hebrews.

Papias, according to Eusebius, also used it, for he quotes from it the story of the woman taken in adultery.

Irenæus (Hœr. i. 26) tells us that the Ebionites (Church of Jerusalem) used "that Gospel which is according to Matthew." As we have overwhelming evidence that the Ebionites used the Gospel according to the Hebrews, it is plain that the Gospel according to Matthew of Irenæus was the Gospel according to the Hebrews.

Remains Justin Martyr, and now the din of battle grows loud. Did he know anything of the sayings (λόγια)? Had he ever heard of the Gospel according to the Apostles? Or did he, according to the conventional defence, know only our Matthew, Mark, Luke, and John?

The answer on the surface seems convincing. Justin never mentions the Gospels of Matthew, Mark, Luke, or John at all. He makes one hundred and ninety-seven quotations from the Old Testament, with the names of the authors and books attached. He alludes to "a man amongst us named John," as the author of the Revelations. He gives two hundred gospel quotations, and professes to get them from the sayings of our Lord, though he does not mention Matthew. He announces also that he is citing the "Memoirs of the Apostles," the alternative title apparently of the Gospel according to the Hebrews. Are the sayings of our Lord quoted by Justin precisely similar to the words of Christ in our gospels? As a matter of fact, they differ considerably in the English translation, and still more in the Greek, as shown by Dr. Giles in his "Hebrew and Christian Records." It is replied that Justin quoted from our gospels and made mistakes.

Much has been made by the conventional defence of certain words used by Justin in reference to the works he was quoting from, "which are called gospels," but Schliermacher contends that the passage is an interpolation, and an instance in which a marginal note has been incorporated into the text. He urges, and so does Dr. Giles, that, at the date of Justin, ευαγγελια could not have been used in the plural for books. It is twice used in the singular by Justin elsewhere, and then means simply the Christian revelation (literally, glad tidings).

I propose now to give all that can be recovered from the writings of the Fathers of the Gospel according to the Apostles. To this I will add the "Sayings of our Lord" as quoted by Justin. If these are not from the Gospel of the Hebrews, at any rate we get a much earlier version of Christ's words than those read in our churches. For the Gospel according to the Hebrews, consult Renan, "Les Evangiles," chap. vi.; Hilgenfeld, "Novum Testamentum extra Canonem Receptum," Fasc. iv.; Nicholson, "The Gospel according to the Hebrews;" and Baring-Gould.

THE GOSPEL ACCORDING TO THE HEBREWS.

Epiphanius has given us the opening verses:—

"There was a certain man, by name Jesus, and he of about thirty years, who chose us out.

"And when he had come to Capernaum, he entered into the house of Simon, who was surnamed Peter, and opened his mouth and said,

"Passing by the Lake of Tiberias, I chose out John and James, sons of Zebedee, and Simon and Andrew, . . . and Thaddæus, and Simon the Zealot, and Judas the Iscariot;

"And thee, Matthew, sitting at the receipt of custom, I called, and thou didst follow me.

"I will therefore that ye be twelve apostles for a testimony to Israel."

A fragment shows that the flight into Egypt was in the gospel.

". . . then he arose and took the young child and departed into Egypt,

"That it might be fulfilled which was spoken of the prophet, Out of Egypt have I called my son."

Now, supposing that there were no class interests in

the way, it would be difficult to read the opening verses of this gospel without seeing what Justin meant by the "Memoirs of the Apostles." In it the Apostles expressly announce that Jesus has "chosen them out" to produce a "testimony," testament, memorial; and Matthew, apparently, is to be the amanuensis. This "testimony" was the entire New Testament, with the earliest Church, the Church of Jerusalem. It was called indiscriminately, as we have seen from Jerome, the Gospel according to the Apostles, and the Gospel according to Matthew. Papias and Hegesippus, the immediate predecessors of Justin, used it, and Irenæus some years later.

Let us go on with the Gospel of the Apostles.

"And John began baptizing.

"And there came out unto him Pharisees who were baptized, and all Jerusalem.

"And John had a raiment of camel's hair and a leathern girdle about his loins, and his food was wild honey, whereof the taste was that of manna.

"And behold the mother of the Lord and his brethren said to him, John the Baptist baptizeth for remission of sins. Let us go and be baptized by him.

"But he said to them, Wherein have I sinned that I should go and be baptized by him? except, perchance, this very thing that I have said is ignorance.

"And when the people had been baptized, Jesus also came and was baptized by John.

"And as he went up, the heavens were opened, and he saw the Holy Spirit, in shape of a dove, descending and entering into him.

"And a voice from heaven said, Thou art my beloved Son. I have this day begotten thee.

"And straightway a great light shone around the place. And John fell down before him, and said, I pray thee, Lord, baptize thou me.

"But he prevented him, saying, Let be; for thus it is becoming that all things be fulfilled.

"And it came to pass when the Lord had come up from the water, the entire fountain of the Holy Spirit descended and rested upon him, and said to him,

"My Son, in all the prophets did I wait thee, that thou mightest come and I might rest in thee;

"For thou art my rest. Thou art my first-born Son for ever and for ever."

"And the Lord said, If thy brother hath sinned in word, and hath made thee amends seven times in a day, receive him.

"Simon, his disciple, said to him, Seven times in a day?

"The Lord answered and said unto him, I tell thee also unto seventy times seven, for in the prophets likewise after they were anointed by the Holy Spirit utterance of sin was found."

"And there was a man whose right hand was withered, and he said, I was a mason, seeking sustenance by my hands. I beseech thee, Jesus, that thou restore me to health that I may not shamefully beg for food. And Jesus healed him.

"And it was told to him, Behold thy mother and thy brethren stand without.

"And he answered, Who is my mother and brethren?

"And he stretched out his hand over the disciples, and said, These are my brethren and mother that do the wishes of my Father.

"And behold there came to him two rich men. And one said, Good master.

"But he said, Call me not good, for he that is good is one, the Father in the heavens.

"The other of the rich men said to him, Master, what good thing shall I do and live?

"He said unto him, Man, perform the law and the prophets.

"He answered him, I have performed them.

"He said unto him, Go, sell all that thou hast and divide it with the poor, and come, follow me.

"But the rich man began to scratch his head, and it pleased him not.

"And the Lord said unto him, How sayest thou, I have performed the law and the prophets? seeing that it is written in the law Thou shalt love thy neighbour as thyself. And behold many of thy brethren, sons of Abraham, are clad with dung, dying for hunger, and thy house is full of much goods, and there goeth from it nought unto them.

"And he turned and said to Simon, his disciple, sitting by him, Simon, son of John, it is easier for a camel to enter through the eye of a needle than a rich man into the kingdom of the heavens."

THE "SAYINGS OF OUR LORD." (Justin Martyr.)

"Love your enemies. Be kind and merciful as your heavenly Father is.

"To him that smiteth thee on the one cheek offer also the other, and him that taketh away thy cloak or thy coat forbid not. And whosoever shall be angry shall be in danger of the fire. And every one that compelleth thee to go with him a mile follow him two. And let your good works shine before men, that they, seeing them, may glorify your Father which is in heaven.

"Give to him that asketh, and from him that would borrow, turn not away. For if ye lend to them of whom ye hope to receive, what new thing do ye? Even the publicans do this. Lay not up for yourselves treasures upon earth, where moth and rust corrupt, and where thieves break through, but lay up for yourself treasure in heaven, where neither moth nor rust doth corrupt. For what is a man profited if he gain the whole world and lose his own soul? And what shall a man give in exchange for it? Lay up, therefore, treasure in heaven, where neither moth nor rust doth corrupt.

"Thou shalt love the Lord thy God with all thy heart, and with all thy strength, and thy neighbour as thyself.

"Swear not at all, but let your yea be yea, and your nay, nay; for whatsoever is more than this cometh of evil.

"If ye love them that love you, what new thing do ye? For even fornicators do this. But I say unto you, pray for your enemies, and love them that hate you, and bless them that curse you, and pray for them that despitefully use you.

"There are some who have been made eunuchs of men

and some who were born eunuchs, and some who have made themselves eunuchs for the kingdom of heaven's sake; but all cannot receive this saying.

"If thy right eye offend thee, cut it out; for it is better for thee to enter the kingdom of heaven with one eye than having two eyes to be cast into everlasting fire.

"Whoso looketh on a woman to lust after her committeth adultery with her already in his heart before God.

"Whoso shall marry that is divorced from another husband committeth adultery.

"I am not come to call the righteous, but sinners to repentance.

"Fear not them that kill you and after that can do no more, but fear him who after death is able to cast both soul and body into hell.

"Except ye be born again, verily ye shall not enter the kingdom of heaven.

"The children of this world marry and are given in marriage, but the children of the world to come neither marry nor are given in marriage, but shall be like the angels in heaven.

"Many false Christs and false apostles shall arise and shall deceive many of the faithful.

"Beware of false prophets, who shall come to you clothed outwardly in sheep's clothing, but inwardly they are ravening wolves.

"And he overthrew the money-changers, and exclaimed, Woe unto ye scribes and Pharisees, hypocrites, because ye pay tithe of mint and rue but do not observe the love of God and justice. Ye whited sepulchres, appearing beautiful outwardly, but are within full of dead men's bones. Woe unto ye scribes, for ye have the keys, and ye do not enter in yourselves, and them that are entering in ye hinder. Ye blind guides, ye are become twofold more the children of hell.

"The law and the prophets were until John the Baptist. From that time the kingdom of heaven suffereth violence, and the violent take it by force.

"And if you can receive it, he is Elijah who was to come. He that hath ears to hear let him hear.

"Elijah must come and restore all things. But I say unto you, Elijah is already come, and they knew him not, but have done to him whatever they chose. Then the disciples understood that he spake to them about John the Baptist.

"The Son of Man must suffer many things, and be rejected by the Pharisees and scribes, and be crucified, and the third day rise again.

"Not every one who saith to me, Lord, Lord, shall enter into the kingdom of heaven, but he that doeth the will of my Father which is in heaven. For whosoever heareth me and doeth my sayings, heareth him that sent me. And many will say unto me, Lord, Lord, have we not eaten and drunk in thy name and done wonders? And then will I say unto them, Depart from me, ye workers of iniquity. Then shall be wailing and gnashing of teeth, when the righteous shall shine like the sun, and the wicked are sent into everlasting fire. For many shall come in my name clothed outwardly in sheep's clothing, but inwardly being ravening wolves. By their works ye shall know them. Every tree that bringeth not forth good fruit is hewn down and cast into the fire.

"I give you power to tread on serpents and on scorpions and on scolopendras, and on all the might of the enemy.

"They shall come from the East and shall sit down with Abraham and Isaac and Jacob in the kingdom of heaven. But the children of the kingdom shall be cast into outer darkness.

"There is none good but God only, who made all things.

"No man knoweth the Father but the Son, nor the Son but the Father, and they to whom the Son revealeth him.

"An evil and adulterous generation seeketh after a sign, and no sign shall be given it save the sign of Jonah.

"Render to Cæsar the things that are Cæsar's, and unto God the things that are God's.

"In whatsoever things I shall apprehend you, in those also will I judge you."

SAYINGS FROM THE GOSPEL ACCORDING TO THE HEBREWS.

"I have come to abolish sacrifices; and if ye do not cease to sacrifice, the wrath of God against you will not cease.

"Be ye approved money-changers.

"No servant can serve two masters. If we wish to serve both God and Mammon it is unprofitable to us.

"I am not come to take away from the law of Moses, nor add to the law of Moses am I come.

"It is blessed to give rather than to receive.

"Keep the mysteries for me and for the sons of my house.

"I am not come to call the just, but sinners.

"There is not thank to you if ye love them that love you; but there is thank to you if ye love your enemies and them that hate you.

"For there shall be false Christs, false prophets, false apostles, heresies, lovings of rule.

"Not every one that saith to me, Lord, Lord, shall be saved, but he that doeth righteousness.

"If ye have been gathered with me into my bosom, and do not my commandments, I will cast you away and will say unto you, Depart from me, I know not whence ye are, workers of iniquity.

"And the Lord said, Ye shall be as lambkins in the midst of wolves. And Peter answered and said, If then the wolves rend the lambkins asunder? Jesus said to Peter, Let not the lambkins after they are dead fear the wolves. And do ye not fear them that kill you and can do nought unto you. But fear him who, after you are dead, hath authority over soul and body to cast into the Gehenna of fire.

"Just now my mother, the Holy Spirit, took me by one of my hairs and bore me up to the great mountain of Tabor.

"He that hath marvelled shall reign, and he that hath reigned shall rest.

"I am he concerning whom Moses prophesied, saying, A prophet will the Lord our God raise unto you from your brethren even as me. Him hear ye in all things, for whosoever heareth not that prophet shall die."

Here is the account of the woman taken in adultery afterwards borrowed by John:—

"And they went each to his own house, and Jesus went to the Mount of Olives.

"And at dawn he came again into the temple, and all the people came to him; and having sat down, he taught them.

"And the scribes and the Pharisees brought up a woman taken up for adultery.

"And having placed her in the midst, they said to him, Teacher, this woman hath been taken up in adultery, in the very act;

"And in the law Moses commanded us to stone such. What therefore dost thou say?

"And this they said, trying him, that they might have whereby to accuse him.

"But Jesus having bent down, kept writing with his finger upon the ground.

"But as they continued asking him, he unbent and said to them, Let the sinless one of you first cast against her the stone. And having bent down again he kept writing on the ground.

"But they having heard, went out one by one, beginning from the elder ones, and Jesus was left alone with the woman.

"And Jesus having unbent, said to her, Mistress, where are they? Hath none condemned thee?

"And she said, None, sir. And Jesus said, Neither will I condemn thee, go and from this time sin no more."

The evidence accumulates. Justin gives the voice

from the sky exactly as it is given in the Gospel of the Apostles.

"Thou art my son. This day have I begotten thee."

He then proceeds to argue against an heretical theory that these words meant that Jesus was the Son of God on receipt of the Holy Spirit at baptism, and not before. But that is plainly the meaning of the passage, for the Ebionites "assert," says Hippolytus, "that our Lord was a man in like sense with all." (L. vii. 2). This is so patent that our first gospel has changed the words to "in thee I am well pleased." Had Justin known the false Matthew's false version, he would have quoted it eagerly instead of taking the trouble to refute the heretics.

I come to a second piece of evidence. In the lives of Krishna, Râma, Buddha, etc., many incidents are plainly inserted as authority for rites. Thus Buddha has his hair cut off by the god Indra, and receives the Abhisheka (baptism) at the hands of the heavenly host; and true Buddhists are expected to imitate him in this. The baptism of the early church was called φωτισμός (Illumination), Justin tells us; and in the Coptic Church, as in Buddhism, the lighting of a taper is still a part of the ceremony. Now Justin informs us that a light was kindled on the Jordan on the occasion of Christ's baptism. It is plain again here that he is quoting from the Gospel according to the Apostles, and not from our gospels, who have cut out this light altogether.

Here is another strong piece of evidence. The Gospel according to the Apostles had a passage about "false Christs, false prophets, false *apostles*." Justin also has a passage about "false Christs, false *apostles*." This is most important, as it refers to St. Paul. Renan shows that in the original Gospel according to the Hebrews, there must have been more than one attack on this "false apostle." He is "the enemy" who sowed tares amongst the gospel wheat. The "enemy" was his nickname with the Church of Jerusalem. Pseudo Matthew softens this to "the devil," and cuts out the "false apostle" altogether. It is plain that Justin is not quoting from him.

Renan refers to another attack on St. Paul from the Gospel according to the Hebrews.

"People have prophesied and cast out devils in the name of Jesus. Jesus openly repudiates them, because they have "practised illegality." (Les Evangiles, chap. vi.)

Stronger still is this. Justin records that when the question was put to Christ, "Show us a sign!" he answered, "An evil and adulterous generation seeketh after a sign, and no sign shall be given them, save the sign of Jonah." Justin goes on to say that Jesus "spoke this obscurely" (Trypho, ch. vii.), and he explains the meaning of the sign. Had he possessed our Matthew, he could not possibly have done this, for in the 40th verse of the twelfth chapter, Jesus, instead of "speaking obscurely," explains that Jonah's three days' sojourn in the whale's belly typifies his own three days' sojourn in the tomb.

In many other points Justin's "Memoirs of the Apostles" differ from our gospels.

"For an ass's foal was standing at a certain entrance

to a village, tied to a vine." Our gospels know nothing about the vine incident when they narrate the story of Christ's entry to Jerusalem. Justin says that Jesus wrought amongst yokes and ploughs. Of this our gospels know nothing.

He says, too, that Jesus was born in a cave. (Trypho, ch. lxxviii.) The First Gospel of the Infancy confirms him here.

"The Magi *from Arabia* came to Bethlehem and worshipped the child." (H. Trypho, ch. lxxviii.) Here again Justin is plainly using some other gospel. Our gospels know nothing of the Magi coming from Arabia.

There is one passage used in the conventional defence to show that Justin knew the fourth gospel also, but Dr. Abbott, in the "Encyclopædia Britannica," holds that this is impossible.

"Except ye be born again, verily ye shall not enter the kingdom of heaven."

It is so obvious that baptism is a new birth, that the Brahmins have been the "twice born" from time immemorial. The Buddhist Abhisheka too is called the "whole birth." Baptism must have been compared to a birth in the young Christian Church from an early date. And if Justin had known Christ's explanations about the birth from water and the Spirit, he could have scarcely wandered on like this. "Now, that it is impossible for those who have once been born to re-enter the wombs of those that bear them, is evident to all."

But there is a more overwhelming argument. Justin was a Platonic philosopher converted to Christianity, as he thought. But in the view of the sober Dr. Lamson, he brought with him into the fold Philo's doctrine of the Logos. It does not appear in Christianity until his date. This Logos, according to Justin and to Philo, was a distinct being, a second God. And in Justin's dialogue with Trypho, he tries to prove all this, enlisting three times into his argument the passage, "No man knoweth the Father but the Son." (Varied in Matt. xi. 27). Is it conceivable that if he had had at his command the opening verses of the fourth gospel, and believed them to be by an apostle of Christ, he would have spared Trypho the infliction of them? The poor Jew would have heard of nothing else.

But a new witness has surged up, coming, as it were, from the tomb. I allude to the fragment of the Gospel of Peter. Justin writes:—

"For also, as said the prophet, mocking him, they placed him on a *tribunal*, and said, Give judgment to us." Our gospels know nothing of the incident of the *tribunal*, nor of the mocking speech recorded by Justin. "Let him who raised the dead save himself." Now, the newly-discovered Gospel of Peter says that they did place Christ on the judgment-seat in mockery. It affirms also at the end that it was inspired by the twelve disciples, just like the Gospel of the Hebrews.

In point of fact, the traditional argument of the advocates of the miraculous origin of our four gospels goes practically on the hypothesis that only these four gospels were in existence in Justin's time. But Dr. Giles shows that Christendom at this period was flooded with spurious gospels, spurious "revelations," spurious "epistles." He cites from Lucian an account of a contemporary of Justin, one Peregrinus, who murdered his father.

"Consigning himself to exile, he took to flight, and wandered about from one country to another. At this time it was that he learnt the wonderful philosophy of the Christians, having kept company with their priests and scribes in Palestine. And what was the end of it? In a short time he showed them to be mere children, for he became a prophet, a leader of their processions, the marshaller of their meetings, and everything in himself alone.

"And of their books, he explained and cleared up some, and wrote many himself; and they deemed him a god, made use of him as a legislator, and enrolled him as their patron." ("Hebrew and Christian Records," p. 82.)

Irenæus bears the same testimony. "But in addition to these things, they introduce an unspeakable number of apocryphal and spurious writings, which themselves have forged, to the consternation of those that are foolish, and who do not know the writings of the truth." (Hœr. i. 19.)

But worse than the composition of imaginery gospels is the falsification of canonical scriptures. "It is obvious," says Origen, "that the difference between the copies is considerable, partly from conclusions of individual scribes, partly from the impious audacity of some in correcting what is written, partly, also, from those who add or remove what seems good to them in the work of correction." (Origen in Matt. xv. 14.)

It might be imagined that a gospel that gives to us the only authentic record of Christ's words, written down at an early date under the sanction of James, Christ's immediate successor as the head of his Church and of the other Apostles, would be cherished in Christendom as the holiest of treasures. Instead of that, it was garbled, truncated, vilified, pronounced heretical by a Pope, and finally suppressed. Why was this? This question is the crux of historical Christianity.

At present we must content ourselves with a brief analysis of the gospel, and say a few words first about the Ebionites.

The word "Ebionite" signifies "poor," and seems to be the Greek rendering of bhikshu or beggar, the word by which Buddha described his followers. The Ebionites were the earliest Christians. They composed the Church of Jerusalem. It fled to Pella, on the Jordan, just before the destruction of the Holy City. Bishop Lightfoot calls them the Essene-Ebionites, because they were plainly in all their rites simple Essenes.

The early fathers gave them five distinctive characteristics:—

1. They held Jesus to be "a man in like sense with all," as we have seen from Hippolytus.

2. They rejected the writings of Paul, and indeed all other New Testament scriptures, except the Gospel according to the Hebrews.

3. They refused to eat meat, like the Essenes.

4. Like the Essenes also they rejected wine, even in the Sacramentum. "Therefore do these men re-

ject the co-mixture of the heavenly wine, and wish it to be the water of the world only, not receiving God so as to have union with him," says Irenæus (Hœr. v. 3) speaking of them.

5. Like the Essenes they also insisted on the rite of circumcision. Here is another passage from Irenæus, "They use the Gospel according to Matthew only, and repudiate the Apostle Paul, maintaining that he was an apostate from the law. As to the prophetical writings, they endeavour to expound them in a somewhat singular manner. They practice circumcision, persevere in the observance of those customs which are enjoined by the law, and are so Judaic in their style of life that they even adore Jerusalem as if it were the House of God." (Hœr. iii. 1.) Irenæus says also that their opinions were similar to those of Cerinthus, who held that Jesus was the son of Joseph and Mary, and that at his baptism the Holy Spirit came to him.

These are the main peculiarities of the Ebionites, and they seem on the surface to show that if Christ was an Essene, and James was an Essene, and their Church after 150 years were still orthodox Essenes, the "heresy" should be sought elsewhere. But at present we will consider the Gospel according to the Apostles.

Epiphanius writes thus:—

"And they have the Gospel according to Matthew very full in Hebrew. For assuredly this is still kept amongst them as it was at outset written in Hebrew letters. But I do not know whether at the same time they have taken away the genealogies from Abraham to Christ." (Hœr. xxix. 9.)

This lets in a flood of light. The main "heresy" of the Gospel according to the Hebrews is that it contains no genealogies. But the same must be said of Mark and John. And there is a version of Luke that was used by the Marcionites that was also without the genealogies. And critics affect to show that our Luke was plainly once without them also:—

"And the Holy Ghost descended in a bodily shape, like a dove, upon him; and a voice came from heaven, which said, Thou art my beloved Son; in thee I am well pleased. And Jesus being full of the Holy Ghost, returned from Jordan, and was led by the Spirit into the wilderness."

This is a consecutive sentence, and yet the genealogies have been clumsily pitchforked into the middle of it. (Luke iii. 23.)

And with regard to Matthew, it can, at least, be proved that Justin Martyr knew nothing of his genealogies.

"He was the Son of Man, either because of his birth by the Virgin, who was, as I said, of the family of David, and Jacob, and Isaac, and Abraham." Plainly Justin thought that it was the Virgin and not Joseph that had descended from Abraham.

But the suppressing of genealogies that were not invented until one hundred years after the Apostles were slumbering in forgotten tombs, was only a detail of their "heresy." Their gospel makes out Christ to be not the Logos masquerading in a human form, but a man and a prophet. "A prophet will the Lord our God raise up unto you from your brethren," he says. And prophets can sin, and he can sin, for he was plainly without the Holy Ghost until his baptism. It comes down, in the Hebrew gospel, not *upon*, but *into* him. And he is the Son of God from that moment, not before.

"Call me not good, for he that is good is one the Father in the heavens!" Pseudo-Matthew weakens this considerably, "There is none good but one, that is God."

"He that is good is one." That was the motto of the Essenes of Jerusalem. Tertullian tells us that certain "unlearned" Christians in his day protested against the Trinity. "They declare that we proclaim two or three gods, but they, they affirm, worship only one." (Adv. Prax. c. 3.) The unlearned were the Church of Jerusalem that still clung to the text, "He that is good is One."

We come to other "heresies." The early gospel knew nothing of Matthew's interpolation about John the Baptist eating locusts, because John the Baptist, as an Essene, could do nothing of the sort. And Jerome tells us that the wicked Ebionites garbled the passage, Luke xxii. 15, to make it appear that Jesus actually refused to eat flesh at the Passover supper.

This is all that can be restored of this in the Ebionite gospel:—

". . . Where wilt thou that we prepare for thee to eat the Passover?"

To this, Jesus answers:—

"Have I desired with desire to eat this flesh, the Passover, with you?"

It is very plain here that Luke is the garbler.

Still more instructive is the question of wine at the

Lord's Supper. Of course, the genuine gospel being written by water drinkers, had no passage about the "fruit of the vine." But Luke, fortunately, has two accounts of the celebration in chap. xxii.

"And he took the cup and gave thanks, and said, Take this and divide it amongst yourselves.

"For I say unto you I will not drink of the fruit of the vine until the kingdom of God has come.

"And he took bread and gave thanks, and brake it, and gave it to them, saying, This is my body which is given for you. This do in remembrance of me.

"Likewise the cup after supper, saying, This cup is the new testament in my blood, which is shed for you."

Now it is perfectly plain that verses 17 and 18 have been clumsily added. They are not in Marcion's version. Mark and Matthew have been more clever. They have garbled the passage better. Verses 19 and 20 fairly represent, I think, the real Gospel of the Hebrews. Justin says that in the "Memoirs of the Apostles," were these words :—

"This do ye in remembrance of me. This is my body!"

In the scene of the Lord's Supper, James was apparently the most prominent character. His removal from the list of the twelve apostles in the canonical gospels is significant.

"And when the Lord had given his shroud to the servant of the priest, he went to James and appeared to him.

"For James had sworn that he would not eat bread from the hour wherein he had drunk the cup of the Lord until he saw him rising again from the dead.

"And the Lord said, Bring a table and bread.

"And he took the bread, and blessed and broke, and afterwards gave it to James the Just, and said, My brother, eat thy bread, for the Son of Man is risen from them that sleep."

Now, the suppression of all this in the orthodox gospels is, as Renan shows, of immense importance. ("Les Evangiles," ch. vi.)

"Then was he seen by James," says St. Paul (1. Cor. xv. 7), "then by all the Apostles."

This shows that the incident was known to the very earliest Church.

CHAPTER VII.

The Essene Jesus.

We now come to an important question, Did Christianity emerge from Essenism?

Historical questions are sometimes made more clear by being treated broadly. Let us first deal with this from the impersonal side, leaving out altogether the alleged words and deeds of Christ, Paul, etc. Fifty years before Christ's birth there was a sect dwelling in the stony waste where John prepared a people for the Lord. Fifty years after Christ's death there was a sect in the same part of Palestine. The sect that existed fifty years before Christ was called Essenes, Therapeuts, Gnostics, Nazarites. The sect that existed fifty years after Christ's death was called "Essenes or Jesseans," according to Epiphanius, Therapeuts, Gnostics, Nazarites, and not Christians until afterwards.

Each had two prominent rites: baptism and what Tertullian calls the "oblation of bread." Each had for officers, deacons, presbyters, ephemereuts. Each sect had monks, nuns, celibacy, community of goods. Each interpreted the Old Testament in a mystical way, so mystical, in fact, that it enabled each to discover that the bloody sacrifice of Mosaism was forbidden, not enjoined. The most minute likenesses have been pointed out between these two sects by all Catholic writers from Eusebius and Origen to the poet Racine, who translated Philo's "Contemplative Life" for the benefit of pious court ladies. Was there any connection between these two sects? It is difficult to conceive that there can be two answers to such a question.

And if it can be proved, as Bishop Lightfoot affirms, that Christ was an anti-Essene, who announced that His mission was to preserve intact every jot and tittle of Mosaism as interpreted by the recognised interpreters, this would simply show that he had nothing to do with the movement to which his name has been given.

There are two Christs in the gospels. Let us consider the Essene Christ first.

The first prominent fact of His life is His baptism by John. If John was an Essene, the full meaning of this may be learnt from Josephus :—

"To one that aims at entering their sect, admission is not immediate; but he remains a whole year outside it, and is subjected to their rule of life, being invested with an axe, the girdle aforesaid, and a white garment. Provided that over this space of time he has given proof of his perseverance, he approaches nearer to this course of life, and partakes of the holier waters of cleansing; but he is not admitted to their community of life. Following the proof of his strength of control, his moral conduct is tested for two years more; and when he has made clear his worthiness, he is then adjudged to be of their number. But before he touches the common meal, he pledges to them in oaths to make one shudder, first that he will reverence the Divine Being, and, secondly, that he will abide in justice unto men, and will injure no one, either of his own accord or by command, but will always detest the iniquitous, and strive on the side of the righteous; that he will ever show fidelity to all, and most of all to those who are in power, for to no one comes rule without God; and that, if he become a ruler himself, he will never carry insolence into his authority, or outshine those placed under him by dress or any superior adornment; that he will always love truth, and press forward to convict those that tell lies; that he will keep his hands from peculation, and his soul pure from unholy gain; that he will neither conceal anything from the brethren of his order, nor babble to others any of their secrets, even though in the presence of force, and at the hazard of his life. In addition to all this, they take oath not to communicate the doctrines to any one in any other way than as imparted to themselves; to abstain from robbery, and to keep close, with equal care, the books of their sect and the names of the angels. Such are the oaths by which they receive those that join them." (Josephus, De B. J., ii. 8, 2, 13.)

As a pendant to this, I will give the early Christian initiation from the Clementine "Homilies."

"If any one having been tested is found worthy, then they hand over to him according to the initiation of Moses, by which he delivered his books to the Seventy who succeeded to his chair."

These books are only to be delivered to "one who is good and religious, and who wishes to teach, and who is circumcised and faithful."

"Wherefore let him be proved not less than six years, and then, according to the initiation of Moses, he (the initiator) should bring him to a river or fountain, which is living water, where the regeneration of the righteous takes place." The novice then calls to witness heaven, earth, water, and air, that he will keep secret the teachings of these holy books, and guard them from falling into profane hands, under the penalty of becoming "accursed, living and dying, and being punished with everlasting punishment."

"After this let him partake of bread and salt with him who commits them to him."

Now if, as is believed by Dr. Lightfoot, the chief object of Christ's mission was to establish for ever the Mosaism of the bloody altar, and combat the main teaching of the ἀσκητής, or mystic, which "postulates the false principle of the malignity of matter," why did He go to an ἀσκητής to be baptised? Whether or not Christ belonged to mystical Israel, there can be no discussion about the Baptist. He was a Nazarite "separated from his mother's womb," who had induced a whole "people" to come out to the desert and adopt the Essene rites and their community of goods. And we see, from a comparison of the Essene and early Christian initiations, what such baptism carried with it. It implied preliminary instruction and vows of implicit obedience to the instructor.

It is plain too that the Essene Christ knows at first nothing of any antagonism to his teacher.

"The law and the prophets were until John. Since that time the kingdom of God is preached, and every man presseth into it." (Luke xvi. 16.)

A rigid continence was exacted :—

"All men cannot receive this saying, save they to whom it is given. . . . There be eunuchs which have made themselves eunuchs for the kingdom of heaven's sake. He that is able to receive it, let him receive it." (Matt. xix. 11, 12.)

"And I looked, and, lo! a Lamb stood on Mount Zion, and with him an hundred and forty-four thousand, having his Father's name written on their foreheads. . . . These are they which were not defiled with women, for they are virgins." (Rev. xiv. 1, 4.)

Divines tell us that this first passage is to have only a "spiritual" interpretation. It forbids not marriage but excess. We might listen to this if we had not historical cognizance of a sect in Palestine at this date which enforced celibacy in its monasteries. The second passage shows that the disciples understood him literally.

The bloody sacrifice forbidden :—

"I will have mercy and not sacrifice." (Matt. ix. 13.)

"Unless ye cease from sacrificing, the wrath shall not cease from you." (Cited from Gospel of the Hebrews by Epiphanius, Hær. xxx. 16.)

Bishop Lightfoot, as I have mentioned, considers that Jesus was an orthodox Jew, whose mission was to perpetuate every jot and tittle of Mosaism; and that "emancipation" from the swathing-bands" of the law came from the Apostles. (Com. on Galatians, pp. 286, 287.) It might be thought that this was a quaint undertaking for the Maker of the million million starry systems to come to this insignificant planet in bodily form to "perpetuate" institutions that Titus in thirty years was to end for ever; even if we could forget that human sacrifices, concubinage, polygamy, slavery, and border raids were amongst these institutions. But if this Christ is the historical Christ, it appears to me that we must eliminate the Christ of the gospels almost entirely. For capital offences against the Mosaic law, the recognised authorities three times sought the life of Jesus, twice after formal condemnation by the Sanhedrim. These offences were Sabbath-breaking, witchcraft, and speaking against Mosaic institutions. According to the Synoptics, he never went to Jerusalem during his ministry until just the end of it; although the three visits for the yearly festivals were rigidly exacted.

In my "Buddhism in Christendom" I give reasons for supposing that the "multitudes" whose sudden appearance in stony wastes have bewildered critics, were in reality the gatherings for the Therapeut festivals described by Philo.

Bishop Lightfoot makes much of the fact that John's gospel makes Christ go up once for the feast of tabernacles. But did he go as an orthodox worshipper, to present his offerings for the bloody sacrifice? On the contrary, on this very occasion he was accused of Sabbath-breaking and demoniac possession; and the rulers of the people sent officers to arrest him.

Leaving Mr. Gladstone and Professor Huxley to discuss whether Christ's acts in the temple among the money changers were illegal, I must point out that His dispersing the sellers of doves goes quite against the theory that He desired to perpetuate Mosaic institutions, for the sale of these doves was a necessity for the temple sacrifices.

Much has been made in modern pulpits of a vague word, "fulfilling." Christ, it is said, did not overthrow the old law, he "fulfilled" it. This is nonsense. Mosaism was an "eternal covenant." It was a "perpetual statute," offerings of the "food of the Deity" on the altar of burnt sacrifice. It was concubinage, slavery, polygamy, the *lex talionis* made eternal institutions. To say that a teacher who preaches forgiveness in place of revenge, continence for concubinage, slaving for, instead of slaving others, immortality of the soul for the religion of to-day, is "fulfilling" merely an abuse of words.

CHAPTER VIII.

The Anti-Essene Jesus.

I HAVE said that in the New Testament there is an Essene and an anti-Essene Christ. Both are most conspicuous in the Gospel of St. Luke. Catholic and Protestant disputants are aware of this.

Until the days of Ferdinand Christian Baur, St. Luke had an immaculate reputation. He was believed to be the companion of St. Paul on his voyages. He was believed to have written the third gospel almost as early as the date of Paul's imprisonment. He was the reputed author of the Acts of the Apostles.

"Luke, the beloved physician, and Demas, greet you." (Col. iv. 14.)

In the Second Epistle to Timothy, and in the Epistle to Philemon, he is also mentioned.

But now all is changed.

In the first place, two out of the three epistles that name him are pronounced to be forgeries by all competent critics; and very few hold even the Epistle to the Colossians to be by the pen of St. Paul. Then it is pointed out that there is no mention of St. Luke's gospel or of the Acts of the Apostles until the date of Irenæus (A. D. 180.)

Let us give the opening verses of the gospel as amended by that eminent Greek scholar, Dr. Giles:—

"Forasmuch as many have taken in hand to set forth in order a narrative of those things which have been brought to fulfilment in us, even as they which from the beginning were eye-witnesses and ministers of the word have handed down to us, it hath seemed good to me also, following all accurately from the beginning, to write unto thee, in order, most excellent Theophilus, that thou mightest know the certainty of those things wherein thou hast been instructed."

Now, here it is plain, as Dr. Giles remarks, that the author "does not profess to have been an original writer, or to have had perfect understanding of all things from the very first," which is the erroneous rendering of our authorised version, but that he follows the accounts of others, who "were eye-witnesses and ministers of the word." (Giles, "Apostolical Records," p. 34.)

Next comes the pertinent question, Who was the "most excellent Theophilus?" The word used is *Kratistos*, "which is thought by Gibbon to designate a man holding a civil or official dignity. If this be so, we might find it difficult to suppose that such a title would have been given to a Christian, even if there were any one of exalted station, within a few years after the first promulgation of Christianity." ("Apostolical Records," p. 13.)

But at Antioch, about the year 171, there was a Theophilus, the sixth bishop. He might have been called Kratistos without anything inappropriate. He was a convert late in life, which may explain the passage about "those things in which thou has been instructed." Eusebius tells us that this Theophilus wrote a treatise against Marcion. But in the view of modern critics, the forged epistles of Paul to Timothy were also levelled against Marcion.

This has its significance. For the followers of Marcion have always maintained that Luke's gospel is Marcion's gospel enlarged and falsified. One of these, Megethius, declared it was full of errors and contradictions. This controversy has been revived in modern times.

But before we deal with this important gospel, we must say a word about what the Germans call Luke's "tendency,"—his scheme of colour, to use an artistic expression.

Baur, comparing the Acts with other scriptures, was struck with the many discrepancies and absolute false statements that it contained. He perceived also that these false statements were not accidental but systematic. Soon their motive dawned upon him. It was plain that this "Luke," writing long after the animosities of Paul against the historical Apostles had ceased, desired to tone down and conceal these animosities. Hence the book of the Acts of the Apostles could not be the work of a contemporary. And a strong motive for this has been suggested by erudite Germans.

The early enemy of Christianity was the Jew. The Roman official at first treated the animosities of the dominant party as part of the incomprehensible Jewish superstition, and sided, when practicable, with the weaker section. But when Christianity began to gain ground, the Roman began to examine it more closely, and soon found much to condemn. For the Essenes proclaimed that the State gods of the Romans were wicked demons. The Essenes forbade the use of wine and flesh meat, important elements in the ceremonial of the Roman religion. The Essenes forbade slavery. The Essenes forbade marriage, replacing it, according to rumour, with lewd rites in their secret orgies. Soon violent persecutions arose.

Now it has been suggested by the Germans that at the date of Kratistos, the school of Antioch sought to conciliate the Roman authority by showing that Christianity was a harmless form of Judaism, equally entitled to State toleration.

This "tendency" of "Luke" must be borne in mind. It is very plain in the earlier chapters of the Acts. The gospels announce that at Christ's death consternation and cowardice were amongst his followers. The "lambs" had fled in all directions from the "wolves." St. Paul also speaks of the fierce persecutions that followed the event,—Stephen stoned, and the "havoc" and the "slaughter." And yet in the opening chapters of the Acts we find the "wolves" more gentle than the "lambs." They are "pricked in their heart." They at once allow Peter to proclaim in the temple, and also before the Sanhedrim, that there is no salvation in any name other than that of the malefactor they have just executed (by inference not even in Yahve); and that all who will not hear this malefactor shall be destroyed. And the Sanhedrim, in solemn conclave, let him go, "finding nothing how they might punish him." (Acts iv. 21.) And Gamaliel, a solemn doctor, advises his colleagues to let the hated "lambs" alone, "lest haply they be found to fight against God." Had a "wolf" talked like that, his brother "wolves" would have made short work of him.

The "tendency" here is very plain. "Luke" wants it to be understood that from the first the chief doctors saw no harm in Christianity, and allowed it to be preached in the temple. I shall not waste time over the controversy, whether "Luke" is an enlargement of Marcion's or some other shorter gospel. As we know that the earliest and only authentic gospel came from the Essene Ebionites, it is plain that all anti-Essenism is an accretion.

We now come to the opening chapters of Luke's gospel. Let us see if it is possible at this distance of time to trace how they were built up.

In the Jerusalem Talmud, and also in the Babylonish, is a somewhat fanciful account of the slaughter of a priest named Zacharias, who was killed in the court of the priests, *near the altar*. A great miracle now occurred: his blood began to bubble, that it might cause fury to come up to take vengeance! Soon Nebuzaradan (this fixes the date of the story to the reign of Nebuchadnezzar) arrived at the temple. He asked the meaning of the bubbling. He was told that the blood was the blood of calves, and rams, and lambs. He caused some calves, and rams, and lambs to be slaughtered; still the blood bubbled. He slaughtered a number of rabbins; still the blood bubbled. Ninety-four thousand priests were slaughtered before the blood of the dead Zacharias was appeased. (Talmud Hierosol. in Taanith, fol. 69, Lightfoot the Hebraist.)

We now come to the Protevangelion, a fanciful gospel attributed to James, the "Bishop of Bishops," as he is called on the title page. It has incorporated this story of Zacharias and his avenging blood; and tacked on to it an account of the birth of the Virgin Mary. One Joachim was much afflicted because Anna his wife had no issue. He "called to mind the patriarch Abraham, how that God in the end of his life had given him his son Isaac," and he went into the wilderness and fasted forty days. An angel appeared to Anna and promised offspring. Mary the child was born, and dedicated to God. Zacharias, the high priest, received her in the temple. When she was twelve years old a veil was wanted, and the high priest cast lots to find out what maiden should spin it. The lot fell on Mary, and from this moment Zacharias was dumb.

Meantime, Mary was espoused to Joseph, who, shortly afterwards finding his betrothed with child, was sorrowful. Both were summoned before the deputy of Zacharias, who caused them to go through the prescribed ordeal of drinking "the water of the Lord." Christ was born. The wise men came. Herod slew the infants, and murdered Zacharias in the temple. Then a mighty miracle occurred. The roofs of the temple howled, and were rent from the top to the bottom. And a voice from heaven said, "Zacharias is murdered, and his blood shall not be wiped away until the revenger of his blood shall come."

Let us now suppose that Luke comes across this story, the "Luke" of the epoch of the most excellent

Theophilus, the Luke with the "tendency" to soften subversive Essenism. How would he proceed? He might argue that John the Baptist would make a more suitable hero. He could be born of old parents like Mary. And the story would certainly gain in unity and dramatic vigour, if Zacharias the priest was made the old father.

That one author has copied from the other there can be no doubt.

Hail, thou art full of grace, thou art blessed amongst women. (Prot. ix. 7.)	Hail, thou art highly favoured. Blessed art thou among women. (Luke i. 28).
Mary, the Lord God hath magnified thy name to all generations. (Prot. vii. 4.)	My soul doth magnify the Lord. Henceforth all generations will call me blessed. (Luke i. 46, 48).
Mary, the Holy Ghost shall come upon thee, and the power of the Most High overshadow thee.	The Holy Ghost shall come upon thee, and the power of the Highest overshadow thee.
Wherefore, that which shall be born of thee shall be holy, and shall be called the Son of the Living God.	Therefore, also that holy thing which shall be born, shall be called the Son of God. (Luke i. 35.)
And thou shalt call his name Jesus. (Prot. ix. 13.)	And shalt call his name Jesus. (Luke i. 31.)
For lo, as the voice of thy salutation reached my ears, that which is in me leaped and blessed me. (Prot. ix. 21.)	And it came to pass when Elizabeth heard the salutation of Mary, the babe leaped in her womb. (Luke ii. 41.)

The question now arises, Which author has copied from the other? Three theories are possible.

1. "James" copied the story from Luke, the companion of Paul.

2. James copied the story from "Luke," of a later date.

3. Luke copied from James.

1. Bishop Lightfoot is angry that an "evangelist" should be accused of copying from an "apocryphal gospel." But there is the difficulty here, that the Zacharias of both stories is plainly the Zacharias of the Talmudic narrative. So that, if the bishop could prove that "James" had stolen from Luke, there would still be an "apocryphal" document behind both. And if "Luke" was the first to use the Talmudic story, how is it that he misses the point of that story, and James copying him, hits it? That point is the avenging blood.

2. The details of the picture and the whole local colour point plainly to an age when past events have so faded away from the memory of living people that a writer can afford to play tricks with them. The huge animosity with which dominant Israel viewed spiritual Israel would have made even Torquemada feel lukewarm. Christ called the two the "wolves" and the "lambs." And yet a chief "wolf," on being informed that his son is to be a water-drinking Nazarite, a leader of the abominable schismatics who prated about the "power of Elias," and called themselves a "people prepared for the Lord," feels ecstasy rather than wrath. Imagine Philip of Spain learning that a son of his had helped to steer the English fire-ships at the great battle of Gravelines. Imagine Legree composing an original song of triumph on learning that Uncle Tom was a free citizen. If there was a historical Luke, and he was the genuine companion of Paul, he of all men would know of the "haling men and women and committing them to prison," of the "havoc and the

slaughter." He would have known how the priestly party in Jerusalem would view a proposal to annul the eternal covenant of Yahve with a better, a more "holy covenant," and substitute remission of sins by penitence for remission of sins by the bloody sacrifice.

3. If the opening chapters of Luke are historical, many events in his own and the other gospels are plainly unhistorical. If John the Baptist was the cousin of Christ, brought up with him from childhood, how is it that he failed to recognise him on the Jordan (John i. 33) until the First Person of the Trinity intervened, and performed the miracle of sending down a dove to indicate him? Why, too, should he have sent, as Luke himself announces (vii. 19), messengers to his cousin to ask if he was the coming Messiah, when he must have known from his mother the announcement of the angels that his cousin was the "Son of the Highest," destined to "reign over Jacob for ever"? Why, too, did Mary, knowing all this, forget it when the boy-Christ disputed in the temple? and why did Luke forget it too? (Luke ii. 48.)

4. If John the Baptist was really the son of a chief priest, the silence of the other gospels is unaccountable. Certainly if Justin Martyr had had the opening chapters of Luke before him, he would have used them against Trypho.

5. When I first read Luke critically, I asked myself, Why has he omitted the death of Zacharias, as he has dragged him in? Then I was struck with the words that he has put into the mouth of Christ :—

"From the blood of Abel to the blood of Zacharias

which *perished between the altar and the temple.*" (Ch. xi. 51.)

This passage convinced me that he had the Protevangelion before him. It is to be remarked that this verse does not appear in Marcion's version.

Then I came across a whimsical passage in Bishop Lightfoot. He shows that an "early tradition identified the Zacharias who is mentioned in the gospels as having been slain between the temple and the altar (Matt. xxiii. 35) with this Zacharias, the father of the Baptist." ("Supernatural Religion," p. 256.) The bishop then triumphs over the author of "Supernatural Religion," who had declared that Luke makes no announcement of Zacharias's death. "He appears," says Bishop Lightfoot, "to have forgotten Luke xi. 51." (Op. cit. p. 257.)

But surely the bishop has overlooked one whimsical objection to accepting this story as historical. If the John the Baptist was the son of Zacharias, the son of Barachias, he must have been 531 years old when he baptised Christ.

Bishop Lightfoot makes much of these opening chapters, because they show that the parents of Jesus were orthodox Jews, who went up every year to the feast of the Passover, and offered doves at the prescribed times. But what about Herod and the flight into Egypt? If the first four chapters which "Luke" is accused of adding to Marcion's gospel be historical, the flight into Egypt is a fiction.

The Buddhist story about Simeon, and the Buddhist disputation with the doctors, are borrowed from the First Gospel of the Infancy. They are not in any other canonical gospel, and the First Gospel of the Infancy is the great armoury of Buddhist legends.

It is to be remarked that a young Buddhist, that he may acquire readiness in controversy, is pestered with questions by doctors and theologians. But the rabbis at Jerusalem would scarcely have allowed a little boy to talk to them about the Messiah. (First Infancy, xxi. 3.)

We now come to the two passages most relied on by those who desire to show that Jesus condemned the asceticism of John. Let us read each with its context.

"And when the messengers of John were departed, he began to speak unto the people concerning John, What went ye out into the wilderness for to see? A reed shaken with the wind? But what went ye out for to see? A man clothed in soft raiment? Behold, they which are gorgeously apparelled, and live delicately, are in kings' courts. But what went ye out for to see? A prophet? Yea, I say unto you, and much more than a prophet. This is he, of whom it is written, Behold, I send my messenger before thy face, which shall prepare thy way before thee. For I say unto you, Among those that are born of women there is not a greater prophet than John the Baptist, *but he that is least in the kingdom of God is greater than he.* And all the people that heard him, and the publicans, justified God, being baptized with the baptism of John. But the Pharisees and lawyers rejected the counsel of God against themselves, being not baptized of him.

"*And the Lord said, Whereunto then shall I liken the men of this generation? and to what are they like? They are like unto children sitting in the market-place, and calling one to another, and saying, We have piped unto you, and ye have not danced; we have mourned to you, and ye have not wept. For John the Baptist came neither eating bread nor drinking wine; and ye say, He hath a devil. The Son of man is come eating and drinking; and ye say, Behold a gluttonous man, and a wine-bibber, a friend of publicans and sinners!* But wisdom is justified of all her children." (Luke vii. 24-35.)

It is a singular fact that this short passage has been made the chief armoury of the disciples of gastronomic, and also of interior Christianity. Thus Migne's "Dictionnaire des Ascétes" cites it to show that Christ approved of the asceticism of the Baptist. Does not this at starting seem to argue two teachings, and, as a corollary, two distinct teachers? If we omit the passages that I have marked in italics it is difficult to find a more eloquent eulogy of ascetic mysticism. The Buddhist mystics are called the Sons of Wisdom (Dharma or Prajñâ), and Christ adopts the same terminology. Plainly the gist of the passage is that the children of the mystic Sophia have no rivalry and no separate baptism. The lower life of soft raiment and palaces is contrasted with John's ascetic life amongst the "reeds" that still conspicuously fringe the rushing Jordan. John is pronounced the greatest of prophets, and his teaching the "counsel of God." Then comes my first passage in italics, the statement that the most raw catechumen of Christ's instruction is superior to this the greatest of God's prophets. It completely disconnects what follows from what precedes, and involves the silliest inconsequence, as shown by the action of Christ's hearers. It is said that they crowded to the "baptism of John." Had that speech been uttered, of course they would have stayed away from it.

The subsequent insertion of the gospel of eating and drinking, and piping and dancing, involves a greater folly. It betrays a writer completely ignorant of Jewish customs. The fierce enmity of anti-mystical Israel to the Nazarites pivoted on the very fact that the latter were pledged for life to drink neither wine nor strong drink. This was the Nazarite's banner with victory already written upon it. Hence the fierce hatred of the Jewish priesthood. If Christ in their presence had drunk one cup of wine, there would have been no crucifixion, and certainly no upbraiding.

This is the second passage that anti-mystical Christianity builds upon:—

"*And they said unto him, Why do the disciples of John fast often, and make prayers, and likewise the disciples of the Pharisees; but thine eat and drink? And he said unto them, Can ye make the children of the bridechamber fast, while the bridegroom is with them? But the days will come, when the bridegroom shall be taken away from them, and then shall they fast in those days.*

"And he spake also a parable unto them: No man putteth a piece of a new garment upon an old; if otherwise, then both the new maketh a rent, and the piece that was taken out of the new agreeth not with the old. And no man putteth new wine into old bottles; else the new wine will burst the bottles, and be spilled, and the bottles shall perish. But new wine must be put into new bottles; and both are preserved. *No man also having drunk old wine straightway desireth new: for he saith, The old is better.*" (Luke v. 33-39.)

I have again resorted to italics. I think we have here a genuine speech of Christ, and a very important one. His doctrine was "new wine," and it was quite unfit for the "old bottles" of Mosaism. The gravity of this speech was felt by the Roman monks who were trying to force the new wine into the old bottles (with much prejudice to the wine), so they tried to nullify it with flat contradiction let in both above and below.

"For the old is better."

This completely contradicts Christ's eulogy of the Christian's "new wine." Moreover, the words are not found in Matthew's version, which makes the cheat more palpable. There, too, we have the gospel of eating and drinking, a gospel that did not require an avatâra of the Maker of the Heavens for its promulgation.

But supposing that we concede the two passages to be genuine, I do not see that the priests of materialism will gain very much.

These texts are internecine, involving contradictions due either to more than one author, or to an interpolator singularly deficient in logical consistency and common sense. The statement, as far as it is intelligible, is that Christ, having determined to forsake mystical for anti-mystical Israel, made the following enactments:—

1. That the ascetic practices that He had taken over from John the Baptist and the Nazarenes, and which in other gospels He enjoins under the phrase of "prayer and fasting" as the machinery for developing miraculous gifts, interior vision, etc., shall be discontinued by His disciples during His lifetime and then again renewed.

2. That feastings and the use of wine, which as Nazarites He and His disciples had specially forsworn, should be again resumed, with no restrictions in this case in the matter of His death. So that by one enactment His disciples after His death were to remain jovial "wine-bibbers" by the other fasting ascetics. It is scarcely necessary to bring forward the true Luke to confute the pseudo Luke.

A valuable historical transaction is recorded by the real Luke which throws a strong light on the relations between Christ and John the Baptist. Towards the close of the Saviour's career, at Jerusalem itself, the chief priests accosted Him and asked Him by what authority He did what He did. Now if the relations between Christ and John the Baptist had been what the pseudo Luke would have us believe, Christ had only to state all this and He might have saved many valuable lives. He had only to plainly announce that His movement was not from anti-mystical to mystical Israel, but from mystical to anti-mystical Israel; that he had introduced wine and oil as a protest against Essenism; that He had forbidden its ascetic fastings, and brought many disciples back from "the baptism of John" to the orthodox fold. If He had stated all this clearly, the high priest and elders would have hailed Him as a friend instead of slaying Him as a foe. But the Saviour, evidently quite unaware that He had led a great movement against the Baptist, takes refuge behind John instead of condemning him. He asks the pregnant question, Was he a prophet of God, or was he not? inferring, of course, that he was, and that the prophetic gift was "authority" enough. (Luke xx. 1, *et seq.*) "For I say unto you, Among those that are born of women there is not a greater prophet than John the Baptist." (Luke vii. 28.) Here again we have the real Luke confronting his unskilful interpolator.

CHAPTER IX.

The Church of Jerusalem.

COMPETENT critics hold that Luke has based the Acts on earlier records. Certainly the picture of the early Church at Jerusalem is very Essenic. The disciples had all things in common. They lived in groups of houses, with a central house of assembly, like the Therapeuts. They had two main rites, baptism and the breaking of bread. They had for officers, deacons, presbyters, ephemereuts. Wine and flesh meat were forbidden, if we may judge the parent from the daughter. For the Roman Christians before the advent of St. Paul forbade wine and flesh meat, and the Roman Church was the eldest daughter of the Church at Jerusalem. Also we see from the Apocalypse that the saints of the New Jerusalem were "virgins."

Thus history flashes a light, transient but vivid, on the rising religion at three distinct periods.

1. When Christ by the Sea of Tiberias preached the memorable λόγια, and said, "Be eunuchs, sell all worldly goods. Blessed are the poor!"

2. When James started the vegetarian water-drinking celibates of the Church of Jerusalem.

3. When Irenæus attacked the vegetarian water-drinking celibates of the Church of Jerusalem which had migrated to Pella (A.D. 180).

Now, these three flashes of light seem to me to dispel much, notably all disquisitions which seek to combine the Essene Christ and the anti-Essene Christ. Renan holds that the Church of Jerusalem were Pharisees. If so, why had they Essene rites, A.D. 34 and A.D. 181? He admits that these rites were borrowed from the Mendaites, or Disciples of John, and that there is the closest analogy between the rise of Christianity and the rise of "other ascetic religions, Buddhism for example." ("Les Apôtres," pp. 78-90.) He admits that the accounts in the Acts of Peter's bold preachings in the temple, are not to be reconciled with passages about "closed doors for few of the Jews." What has chiefly led to misapprehensions is not so much the dishonesty of writers like "Luke," as the fiction of the Essenes themselves that they were orthodox Jews. They were most particular about circumcision. They had a Sanhedrim of Justice, and so had the early Christians. The Church of Jerusalem had its "chief priest," as we see from the First Epistle of Clement to the Corinthians. "The daily sacrifices are not offered everywhere, nor the peace-offerings, nor the sacrifices appointed for sins and transgressions, but only at Jerusalem, nor in any place there, but only at the altar before the temple." (Ch. xviii.)

This chief priest must not be confused with the Jewish one. He has been established by God through Christ. (Ch. xix. 7.) It is also stated that Christ has laid down what "offerings and service" must be performed. (Ch. xviii. 14.) This gives a significance to the passages in Revelations describing the temple of the mystic Jerusalem, which would of course be modelled on the "temple" familiar to the white-robed virgin saints of the material New Jerusalem, the "angel" taking the "golden censer" and filling it with the fire of the altar, the "lamps," the "candlesticks," the "golden altar," the "incense." The ground near Jerusalem is perforated with caverns. This temple, probably, was some secret crypt like a chapel in the catacombs. Keim points out that the command given in chap. xi. verse 2 of the Revelations to leave out the court of the bloody sacrifices in the ideal temple of the New Jerusalem, is an additional piece of evidence in favour of the Essenism of the early Church.

This is what Hegesippus, the earliest Christian historian, says about James, described in the Protevangelion as the "chief apostle and first Christian bishop."

"He was consecrated from his mother's womb. He drank neither wine nor strong drink, neither ate he any living thing. A razor never went upon his head. He anointed not himself with oil, nor did he use a bath. He alone was allowed to enter into the holies. For he did not wear woollen garments, but linen. And he alone entered the sanctuary and was found upon his knees praying for the forgiveness of the people, so that his knees became hard like a camel's through his constant bending and supplication before God, and asking for forgiveness for the people." (Eusebius, "Hist. Eccl." ii. 33.)

This passage seems to settle the question whether the early Christians were Essenes or Pharisees.

Here we have the chief apostle depicted as an Essene of Essenes. He rejects wine and flesh meat. And the "temple" of the Essenes was plainly not the Jewish temple. The temple guards would have made short work of any one rash enough to attempt to enter the Holy of Holies.

Epiphanius adds the two sons of Zebedee to the list of the ascetics, and also announces that James, the chief apostle, entered the Holy of Holies once a year. He gives another detail, that the Christian bishop wore the bactreum or metal plate of the high priest. (Epiph. Hær. lxxviii. 13, 14.)

Clement of Alexandria gives a similar account of St. Matthew:—

"It is far better to be happy than to have a demon dwelling in us. And happiness is found in the practice of virtue. Accordingly, the Apostle Matthew partook of seeds, and nuts, and vegetables without flesh." (Pædag. ii. 1.)

The Clementine "Homilies" give a far more authentic picture of the Church of Jerusalem than the Acts. In them St. Peter thus describes himself:—

"The Prophet of the Truth who appeared on earth taught us that the Maker and God of all gave two kingdoms to two (beings), good and evil, granting to the evil the sovereignty over the present world. . . . Those men who choose the present have power to be rich, to revel in luxury, to indulge in pleasures, and to do whatever they can; for they will possess none of the future goods. But those who have determined to accept the blessings of the future reign have no right to regard as their own the things that are here, since they belong to a foreign king, with the exception only of water and bread and those things procured with sweat to maintain life (for it is not lawful to commit suicide); and also only one garment, for they are not permitted to go naked." (Clem. Hom. xv. 7.)

A word here about the "Sepher Toldoth Jeshu," a work which orthodoxy as usual would modernise overmuch. It is a brief sketch of Christ's life, and, at any rate, represents the Jewish tradition of that important event. It announces that the Saviour was hanged on a tree for sorcery. After that there was a bitter strife between the "Nazarenes" and the "Judeans." The former, headed by Simeon Ben Kepha, (who, "according to his precept," abstained from all food, and only ate "the bread of misery," and drank the "water of sorrow,") altered all the dates of the Jewish festivals to make them fit in with events in Christ's life. This seems to make Peter and the "Nazarenes" or Nazarites water-drinking vegetarian ascetics.

Old Jerusalem, considered as a religious centre, quite eclipsed holy cities like Benares or mediæval Rome, for the chief rites could only be performed there. The Jewish Christians plainly traded with this exceptional importance, adding a more powerful claim. For in Israel, for at least a hundred years, there had been a strange prophetic book, believed, even by the writer of one Christian scripture (Jude), to be written by the patriarch Enoch. This book was believed to be genuine by Irenæus, Clement of Alexandria, Origen, and Tertullian. For a thousand years it was lost to Christendom, and then Bruce brought back three copies from Abyssinia. Archbishop Laurence translated the work in 1821.

The importance of the Book of Enoch is that it gives quite a new view of the mission of the Messiah. From their prophets the Jews expected a conqueror who was to come with a "bow" and the "sword of the mighty," and to "have dominion from the Jordan to the ends of the earth." That he was to be a mere mortal is proved by the fact that, according to Daniel, he was by-and-by to be "cut off." (Dan. ix. 26.) But the Son of Man of Enoch differed from this:—

"Before the sun and the signs were created, before the stars of heaven were formed, his name was invoked in the presence of the Lord of Spirits. A support shall he be for the righteous and the holy to lean upon, without falling, and he shall be the light of nations.

"He shall be the hope of those whose hearts are troubled. All who dwell on earth shall fall down and worship before him." (Enoch xlviii.)

"Behold he comes with ten thousand of his saints to execute judgment upon them and destroy the wicked." (Enoch ii.) This is the passage cited by Jude.

"In those days shall the earth deliver up from her womb, and hell deliver up from hers, that which it has received, and destruction shall restore that which it owes. He shall select the righteous and holy from among them." (Enoch i.)

"In those days shall the mouth of hell be opened, into which they shall be immerged. Hell shall destroy and swallow up sinners from the face of the elect." (Enoch liv.)

"I beheld that valley in which . . . arose a strong smell of sulphur. . . . Through that valley rivers of fire were flowing." (Enoch lxvi. 5-8.)

"He shall select the righteous and holy from among them, for the day of their salvation has approached." . . . (Enoch l. 2.)

"I saw the habitations and couches of the saints. Then my eyes beheld their habitations with the angels and their couches with the holy ones. Thus shall it be with them for ever and ever." (Enoch xxxix. 4.)

"The former heaven shall depart and pass away, a new heaven shall appear." (Enoch xcii. 17.)

These texts show where the Jews got the idea of a Son of Man coming in the clouds of heaven and summoning the dead from their graves for a great assize. They show where Christianity got its heaven and its hell. The author of the "Evolution of Christianity" gives in parallel columns a number of other passages which seem to have suggested corresponding passages in the Christian scriptures. The defenders of conventional orthodoxy urge that these passages and the passages I have quoted are post-Christian interpolations. In the way of this theory stands the fact that Enoch describes only one advent, that of a superhuman, triumphant Messiah. He knows nothing of a suffering, crucified mortal. That advent, according to the Jewish ideas of the time, seemed at first blush a failure. Surely the first object of an interpolator would have been to suit his prophecies to the double advent, and make the second explain the failure of the first. It is to be observed, too, that Enoch's Son of Man rules in heaven. There is no mention of Jerusalem. It seems very plain that the Apocalypse has attempted to fuse together the Messiah of Enoch and the Messiah of Micah, and the clumsy expedient of a thousand years preliminary rule in Jerusalem, entailing, as it does, two resurrections and two judgment days, is the result.

The Messiah of Enoch is plainly Craosha of the Persians, who will, one day, summon the dead to judgment in their old material bodies, sending the wicked to Douzakh, and the good to Behisht.

Let us see how this affects our present inquiry.

The Buddhists took over from the Brahmins:—

1. A heaven (Swarga) and a purgatory.

2. Ancestor worship (the S'raddha). The Buddhas of the Past had offerings given to them at stated periods at their topes, for which they were expected to perform miracles.

Nothing can be more explicit than the statements in the gospels about the fate of the dead. Souls and bodies are to remain in the festering grave until a trumpet shall sound. Then the body as well as the soul will arise for an universal judgment.

But side by side with this idea soon sprang up a conflicting one, the "Communion of Saints."

"God dwells in the bones of the martyrs," said St. Ephrem, "and by his power and presence miracles are wrought." ("Wiseman's Lectures," xi. 105.) Soon the Buddhist saint worship and the Buddhist purgatory were taken over by the Church, Alexandrian Buddhism fighting with the dualism of Persian Buddhism.

But if there has been no judgment, how can we tell who is in purgatory, and who are the saints? This question seems to have stirred Cardinal Newman, and he attempted an answer in his "Dream of St. Gerontius." Christ has a "rehearsal of judgment." This is, of course, preposterous.

CHAPTER X.

Johannine Buddhism.

THE Indians of old observed that one portion of the sky was dark at night and one portion lit with stars. They judged that the dark portion was spirit—primary substance, and that the light portion was the same substance made tangible to the senses under the form of matter. The Buddhists took over these ideas and called the dark portion Nirvritti and the light portion Pravritti. In Nirvritti dwelt the formless, passionless, inconceivable God—Swayambhu the Self-Existent. Pravritti contained numerous world-systems (Buddha-Kshetras), the Ogdoads of the Gnostics. These christened Nirvritti "Buthos," and Pravritti, the luminous worlds, the "Pleroma." In Buddhism, Pravritti was presided over by five beings, emanations from Swayambhu. These are announced in the Buddhist books to be simply the attributes of Swayambhu personified. They were probably invented to provide the vulgar with a substitute for the old Brahmin hierarchy. Each has a Sakti (wife, female energy). I give a list of them with their Saktis, and the divine attributes that they personify.

ATTRIBUTES.	DHYANI BUDDHAS.	SAKTIS.
Su-vis'uddha Dharma Dhâtu. (Purifying eternal law.)	Vairochana. (Sun-born.)	Vajra Dhateswatî. (Goddess of eternal elements.)
Adarsana. (Invisibility).	Akshobhya. (Immovable.)	Lochanâ. (Eye goddess.)
Prativekshana. (Eyes that sleep not.)	Ratna-Sambhava. (Born of the jewel.)	Mamukhî.
Sânta. (Calmness.)	Amitabha. (Diffusing infinite light.)	Pândarâ. (Pale goddess.)
Krityânushtana. (One who performs rites.)	Amogha-Siddha. (Unfailing aim.)	Târâ. (Star.)

Turning to Basilides we find that he placed in Buthos the "Unnameable," a being similar to Swayambhu. From the Unnameable emanated also five beings, whom he called Æons (Eternals), a substitute for the Dhyani Buddhas. Their names were Nous (Mind), Logos (Speech), Phronesis (Prudence), Sophia (Wisdom), Dunamis (Power).

Plainly these also are simply divine attributes personified, the five Dhyani Buddhas.

Valentinus has also a supreme Æon, Unbegotten, Invisible, Self-Existent, remaining from everlasting in impassive serenity. This God, named Bythus, has his Sakti like the Dhyani Buddhas. She is called Ennœa (Idea), also Charis (Grace).

Bythus is also called Propator (First Father). After countless ages he determines to evolve the Pleroma, and for that purpose brings forth Nous (Mind) and Aletheia (Truth).

From Nous, according to Valentinus, by the aid of

Aletheia proceeded Logos (Word) and Zoe (Life). Nous was also called Monogenes (the Only Begotten).

Zoe brought forth Anthropos (Man) and Ecclesia (Church). These brought forth other Æons.

In this system Christ figures as Phos (Light), Soter (Saviour), and Logos (Word). He gives light to the Pleroma.

Now let us turn to the famous opening verses of the fourth gospel. I copy down the translation of them by the author of the "Evolution of Christianity."

"In the beginning was the Logos, and the Logos was with God, and the Logos was divine. The same was in the beginning with God. All things came into existence through him, and without him nothing came into existence. That which hath been made in him was Zoe (Life), and Zoe was the Phos (Light) of men, and Phos shineth in the darkness, and the darkness apprehended it not. . . .

"And the Logos became flesh, and dwelt amongst us, full of Charis (Grace) and Aletheia (Truth). And we beheld his glory, glory as of Monogenes (the Only Begotten) from the Father."

As the author of the "Evolution of Christianity" truly says, we have here a condensation of the Æons of Valentinus. John unifies Christ in Monogenes, Logos, Phos, and Soter. He descends as Phos (Light). He has Æonic relationship with Charis and Aletheia.

"Of his Pleroma have we all received," says the fourth evangelist. (John i. 16.)

"It was the Father's good pleasure that in him the whole Pleroma should have its home" (Col. i. 19).

"In him dwells the whole Pleroma of the Godhead in bodily shape." (Col. ii. 9).

"The Church, which is his body, the Pleroma of him that filleth all in all." (Eph. i. 23.)

We turn now to the Æons or Dhyani Buddhas.

"According to the purpose of the Æons." (Eph. iii. 11.)

"Even the mystery which hath been hid from ages and from generations."

The author of the "Evolution of Christianity" shows that the authorised version has no sense. He amends it thus:—

"The mystery concealed from the Æons and from their offspring."

From this two things are patent:—

1. Johannine Christianity is Gnosticism.

2. Gnosticism is Buddhism.

In chapter ii. I said that Buddha, like the Gnostic Christ, ruled the Pleroma or Pravritti. In the "Lalita Vistara" many pages are devoted to show that he is Purusha, the God-man of the Hindoos. Purusha is always contrasted with Pracriti, the Buthos of the Gnostics, that part of the Kosmos which is unfashioned and non-luminous. Purusha is like the divine man of the Kabbalah, the Christ of St. Paul, humanity, ideal humanity. Valentinus proclaimed that from Sophia the Mother, proceeded Ecclesia the Church. Jesus called his flock the sons of Sophia, and said that his mother, the Holy Spirit, had carried him up to the top of Mount Tabor.

As early as the Asoka inscriptions the triad of Buddhism was:—

1. Buddha or Swayambhu, the Self-Existent.

2. Dharma or Prajnâ (Sophia).

3. Sangha (literally Union). Sangha "created the worlds," says the Pûja Kanda. (For this triad, see Hodgson, "Lit. Nepal," p. 88.) This triad with the vulgar is now Buddha, his Law, and the Church.

A version of this was not unknown in Palestine, for Hegesippus records of the early Christians:—

"In every city that prevails which the Law, the Lord, and the Prophets enjoin."

CHAPTER XI.

Rites.

I HAVE left myself little space to write of the many points of close similarity between the Buddhists and the Roman Catholics.

The French missionary Huc, in his celebrated travels in Thibet, was much struck with this similarity.

"The crozier, the mitre, the dalmatic, the cope or *pluvial*, which the grand lamas wear on a journey, or when they perform some ceremony outside the temple, the service with a double choir, psalmody, exorcisms, the censer swinging on five chains, and contrived to be opened and shut at will, benediction by the lamas, with the right hand extended over the heads of the faithful, the chaplet, sacerdotal celibacy, Lenten retirements from the world, the worship of saints, fasts, processions, litanics, holy water—these are the points of contact between the Buddhists and ourselves."

Listen also to Father Disderi, who visited Thibet in the year 1714. "The lamas have a tonsure like our priests, and are bound over to perpetual celibacy. They study their scriptures in a language and in characters that differ from the ordinary characters. They recite prayers in choir. They serve the temple, present the offerings, and keep the lamps perpetually alight. They offer to God corn and barley and paste and water in little vases, which are extremely clean. Food thus offered is considered consecrated, and they eat it. The lamas have local superiors, and a superior general." ("Lettres edifiantes," vol. iii., p. 534.)

Father Grueber, with another priest named Dorville, passed from Pekin through Thibet to Patna in the year 1661. Henry Prinsep ("Thibet Tartary, etc.," p. 14) thus sums up what he has recorded:—

"Father Grueber was much struck with the extraordinary similarity he found, as well in the doctrine as in the rituals of the Buddhists of Lha Sa, to those of his own Romish faith. He noticed, first, that the dress of the lamas corresponded with that handed down to us in ancient paintings as the dress of the Apostles. Second, that the discipline of the monasteries and of the different orders of lamas or priests bore the same resemblance to that of the Romish Church. Third, that the notion of an Incarnation was common to both, so also the belief in paradise and purgatory. Fourth, he remarked that they made suffrages, alms, prayers, and sacrifices for the dead, like the Roman Catholics. Fifth, that they had convents filled with monks and friars to the number of thirty thousand, near Lha Sa, who all made the three vows of poverty, obedience, and chastity, like Roman monks, besides other vows. Sixth, that they had confessors licensed by the superior lamas or bishops, and so empowered to receive confessions, impose penances, and give absolution. Besides all this there was found the practice of using holy water, of singing service in alternation, of praying for the dead, and of perfect similarity in the customs of the great and superior lamas to those of the different orders of the Romish hierarchy. These early missionaries further were led to conclude from what they saw and heard that the ancient books of the lamas contained traces of the Christian religion, which must, they thought, have been preached in Thibet in the time of the Apostles."

In the year 1829, Victor Jacquemont, the French botanist, made a short excursion from Simla into Thibet. He writes: "The Grand Lama of Kanum has the episcopal mitre and crozier. He is dressed just like our bishops. A superficial observer at a little distance would take his Thibetan and Buddhist mass for a Roman mass of the first water. He makes twenty genuflexions at the right intervals, turns to the altar and then to the congregation, rings a bell, drinks in a chalice water poured out by an acolyte, intones paternosters quite of the right sing-song—the resemblance is really shocking. But men whose faith is properly robust will see here nothing but a corruption of Christianity." (Corr. vol. i., p. 265.)

It must be borne in mind that what is called Southern Buddhism has the same rites. St. Francis Xavier in Japan found Southern Buddhism so like his own that he donned the yellow sanghâti, and called himself an apostle of Buddha, quieting his conscience by furtively mumbling a little Latin of the baptismal service over some of his "converts."

This is what the Rev. S. Beal, a chaplain in the navy, wrote of a liturgy that he found in China:—

"The form of this office is a very curious one. It bears a singular likeness in its outline to the common type of the Eastern Christian liturgies. That is to say there is a 'Proanaphoral' and an 'Anaphoral' portion. There is a prayer of entrance (τῆς εἰσοδου), a prayer of incense (τοῦ θυμιάματος), an ascription of praise to the threefold object of worship (τρισαγίον), a prayer of oblation (τῆς προσ θεσεως), the lections, the recitations of the Dharanî (μυστηριον), the Embolismus or prayer against temptation, followed by a 'Confession,' and a 'Dismissal.'" ("Catena of Buddhist Scriptures," p. 397.)

Turning to architecture, I must point out that Mr. Ferguson, the leading authority in ancient art, was of opinion that the various details of the early Christian basilica—nave, aisle, columns, semi-domed apse, cruciform ground plan—were borrowed *en bloc* from the Buddhists. Mr. Ferguson lays special stress on the Dâgoba and its enshrined relics, represented in the Christian Church by the high altar, the bones of a saint, the baldechino. Relic worship, he says, was certainly borrowed from the East. Of the rock-cut temple of Kârle (B.C. 78) he writes:—

"The building resembles, to a great extent, an early Christian church in its arrangements, consisting of a nave and side aisles terminating in an apse or semi-dome, round which the aisle is carried. . . . As a scale for comparison, it may be mentioned that its arrangements and dimensions are very similar to those of the choir of Norwich Cathedral, and of the Abbaye aux Hommes at Caen, omitting the outer aisles in the latter buildings.

Immediately under the semi-dome of the apse, and nearly where the altar stands in Christian churches, is placed the Dâgoba. ("Indian and Eastern Architecture," p. 117.)

The list of resemblances is by no means exhausted. The monks on entering a temple make the gesture that we call the sign of the cross. The Buddhists have illuminated missals, Gregorian chants, a tabernacle on the altar for oblations, a pope, cardinals, angels with wings, saints with the nimbus. For a full account I must refer the reader to my "Buddhism in Christendom," where I give (pp. 182, 184) drawings of monks and nuns, the Virgin and Child (p. 205), the adoration of the rice cake on the altar (p. 83), Buddha coming down to the altar with the heavenly host (p. 210), the long candles, artificial flowers, cross, incense burner, and divine figure with the aureole, of the Buddhist temple (p. 208). The election of the Grand Lâma I show to be pin for pin like the election of the Pope. The list is endless.

How is all this to be accounted for? Several theories have been started:—

The first attempts to make light of the matter altogether. All religions, it says, have sacrifice, incense, priests, the idea of faith, etc. This may be called the orthodox Protestant theory, and many bulky books have recently appeared propounding it. But as these books avoid all the strong points of the case, they cannot be called at all satisfactory to the bewildered inquirer.

To this theory the Roman Catholics reply that the similarities between Buddhism and Catholicism are so microscopic and so complete, that one religion must have borrowed from the other. In consequence they try to prove that the rites of Buddhism and the life of its founder were derived from Christianity, from the Nestorians, from St. Thomas, from St. Hyacinth of Poland, from St. Oderic of Frioul. (*See* Abbé Prouvéze, "Life of Gabriel Durand," vol. ii., p. 365.)

In the way of this theory, however, there are also insuperable difficulties. Buddha died 470 years before Christ, and for many years the Christian Church had no basilicas, popes, cardinals, basilica worship, nor even for a long time a definite life of the founder. At the date of Asoka (B.C. 260) there was a metrical life of Buddha (Muni Gatha), and the incidents of this life are found sculptured in marble on the gateways of Buddhist temples that precede the Christian epoch. This is the testimony of Sir Alexander Cunningham, the greatest of Indian archæologists. He fixes the date of the Bharhut Stupa at from 270 to 250 B.C. There he finds Queen Mâyâ's dream of the elephant, the Rishis at the ploughing match, the transfiguration of Buddha and the ladder of diamonds, and other incidents. At the Sanchi tope, an earlier structure (although the present marble gateways, repeated probably from wood, are fixed at about 19 A.D.), he announces representations of Buddha as an elephant coming down to his mother's womb, three out of the "Four Presaging Tokens," Buddha bending the bow of Sinhahanu, King Bimbisâra visiting the young prince, and other incidents.

A man who invents a novel high explosive, or a quick-firing gun, at once puts his idea to a practical test. Let us try and construct a working model here.

Suppose that the present ruler of Afghanistan were paying us a visit, and, introduced at Fulham Palace, he were to suggest that the life of Mahomet should supersede that of Jesus in our Bible, and Mussulman rites replace the Christian ritual in the diocese of London. What would be the answer? The bishop, anxious to deal gently with a valuable ally, would point out that he was only a cogwheel in a vast machinery, a cogwheel that could be promptly replaced if it proved the least out of gear. He would show that the Anglican Church had a mass of very definite rules called canon law, with courts empowered to punish the slightest infringement of these rules. He would show that even an archbishop could not alter a tittle of the gospel narrative. Every man, woman, and child would immediately detect the change.

Similar difficulties would be in the way of St. Hyacinth of Poland in, say, a monastery of Ceylon. The abbot there would be responsible to what Bishop Bigandet calls his "provincial," and he again to his "supérieur général" (p. 478), and so on to the Âchârya, the "High Priest of all the World," who, in his palace at Nalanda, near Buddha Gayâ, was wont to sit in state, surrounded by ten thousand monks. Buddhism, by the time that a Christian missionary could have reached it, was a far more diffused and conservative religion than Anglicanism. It had a canon law quite as definite. It had hundreds of volumes treating of the minutest acts of Sakya Muni.

THE END.

INDEX.